The Neff SlideAway® door does exactly what its name suggests. When you open the oven it slides smoothly away into the compartment below in an effortlessly light action. Which means you can baste and turn food without having to lean over a hot oven door. So you can give the trickiest of dishes all the pampering they deserve. For more information and the recipe for cooking perfect lamb with sage, rosemary and lemon visit neff.co.uk or for a free brochure call 0844 892 9033.

" MY NEW SLIDEAWAY
OVEN DOOR MEANS I
CAN BASTE IT REALLY
EASILY TO KEEP IT JUICY."

writing kitchen history

SPECIAL OFFER

If you've enjoyed the lovely seasonal recipes in the *Jamie Magazine Recipe Yearbook*, you might like to subscribe to *Jamie Magazine* for as little as £18.45 a year – that's a huge saving of 23% on the cover price. Not only this, but if you subscribe by Direct Debit, we'll send you a back issue of *Jamie Magazine*, worth £3.99, completely FREE.

Each issue of *Jamie Magazine* is packed full of more than 120 brilliant recipes from Jamie Oliver and other top chefs around the globe. This beautiful bimonthly mag is a window into Jamie's world – you can cook the dishes that excite him, meet the producers and chefs that inspire him, and discover the destinations he loves to visit. Add in sumptuous photography and thoughtful articles from some of the leading names in the world of food, and you've got a magazine to treasure – and an unmissable package for anyone who appreciates good food, good drink and good times!

There are 3 money-savings options to choose from:

- 1-year subscription via Direct Debit – £18.45 (save 23%)
- 1-year subscription via debit or credit card – £19.95 (6 issues for the price of 5)
- 2-year subscription – £39.50 (12 issues for the price of 10)

You can also give *Jamie* as a gift. Take out a subscription for a friend or relative and each issue will be delivered to their door. If you subscribe by Direct Debit, we'll send you a free back issue (quote 'JMYR09'), so you'll both have something to enjoy.

Looking for inspiration in the kitchen? Start 2010 in style with a subscription to *Jamie Magazine* and you'll have hundreds of wonderful recipes, tips and ideas to keep you cooking all year long

3 EASY WAYS TO SUBSCRIBE

1 Call 0844 249 0478, quoting the code 'JMYR09'. Lines are open 8am–8pm Monday to Friday (9am–1pm Saturday)
2 Log on to jamiemagazine.com/subscribe, entering the code 'JMYR09'
3 Email jamiemagazine@ servicehelpline.co.uk, entering the code 'JMYR09'
Remember, if you subscribe by Direct Debit, we'll also send you a free back issue

WELCOME

YOU'RE HOLDING OUR VERY FIRST YEARBOOK! WORKING WITH the mag team this past year has been a dream come true for me. When I like something I have to shout about it, and having this beautiful magazine has allowed us to share stories about the people and places we think are doing brave and exciting things in the world of food.

This is a collection of our favourite recipes from this first year. Some are mine, others are from the many wonderful contributors we've had, and all are things you'll want to make and enjoy at home again and again.

I hope you love the book. There'll be more great food to come in the year ahead. This is just the beginning...

Editor at Large

JAMIE MAGAZINE WINE CLUB

Here's something to drink to. To celebrate - and complement! - our yearbook, we've got a very special wine offer. Guided by the recipes in this book, we've created a case of 12 great wines, including a champagne and a dessert wine; they're worth £121.88 but you can buy them for just £60.94! Go to page 170 for more details.

It's been an incredibly exciting first year at *Jamie*. Starting any new magazine is a challenge and a privilege but when your founder is Jamie Oliver, you're in for a rollercoaster ride of passionate ideas and inspirational recipes - communicated at all hours. We've had frantic midnight texts about dishes he's just created at home or tasted in far-flung places and wants to share in the issue. Jamie's enthusiasm is infectious and we hope it inspires you in the kitchen as much as it does us.

After testing, tasting and perfecting every new recipe for the magazine in the Jamie Oliver kitchens, we decided to gather some of our favourites together in our first yearbook. They're recipes from Jamie, his food team and chefs from around the world that we think make a stunning collection for cooks (young and old) who might have missed some issues from the first year of *Jamie Magazine*. It's the perfect kitchen companion, full of ideas to feed family and friends - easy starters and snacks, nourishing soups and effortless pastas for midweek meals. Then there are more ideas for formal dinners and plenty of cocktails to get you into a party spirit.

If you're new to our world, see our subscription offer opposite to get *Jamie* delivered to you regularly, or visit jamiemagazine.com for lots more ideas.

Editor

27

9

77

61

129

153

41

97

170

recipe yearbook

Our wine match

Lush Mar de Viñas Albariño is a lovely easy-drinking wine and great with tapas such as pickled quail eggs and guacamole. Go to page 170 for details of our wine offer.

SNACKS & STARTERS

QUICK EATS, PLUS CANAPES FOR WHEN FIRST IMPRESSIONS COUNT

Lots of fast food ideas. Fill your fridge and freezer with stand-bys like pickled quail eggs (page 23), anchovy butter (page 10) and Mrs Yang's potsticker dumplings (page 23). Or take the hassle out of formal dinners with cheats such as ready-made tart cases (page 13) and easy pâtés (page 14)

BEAN & PARSLEY DIP

ANCHOVY BUTTER

BEAN & PARSLEY DIP

- 2 x 400g tins butter beans, drained
- 4 tbsp olive oil
- 2 tbsp chopped flat-leaf parsley
- Juice and grated zest of 1 lemon
- Sliced red onion and grilled bread, to serve

1 Combine butter beans, olive oil, parsley and lemon juice and zest in a food processor. Add generous amounts of salt and pepper and blend to a rough consistency. Transfer to a serving bowl, top with slices of red onion and serve with grilled bread.

ANCHOVY BUTTER

- 250g soft unsalted butter
- 3 tbsp capers, chopped
- 3 tbsp dijon mustard
- 50g finely chopped anchovies

1 Mix butter with capers, mustard, anchovies and a pinch of black pepper. Shape into a large cigar, wrap in baking paper, then refrigerate. This is delicious on hot new potatoes, steamed greens or spread on toast. It will keep in the fridge for up to 2 weeks.

ARANCINI

Makes 24

- 400g arborio rice
- 100g grated parmesan
- 4 eggs, beaten
- 120g gorgonzola dolcelatte, chopped
- 1.5 litres vegetable oil

Coating

- 70g plain flour
- 2 eggs, beaten
- 100g fine breadcrumbs

1 Cook rice in boiling salted water until tender. Drain rice, then transfer to a bowl and combine with parmesan, eggs and salt and pepper to taste. Spread on a large tray, cool, then chill for 2 hours.
2 Place 1 tbsp rice in your palm and flatten slightly. Place 1 tsp gorgonzola in the centre and form the rice around it to make a ball. Repeat with all the rice.
3 For the coating, put the flour, eggs and breadcrumbs in separate bowls. Roll arancini in flour, dip in egg, roll in breadcrumbs, then chill till ready to cook.
4 Heat oil in a large pan to 180C or till a cube of bread turns gold in 30 seconds. (Never leave hot fat unattended.) Very carefully fry arancini, in batches, for 5 minutes or till golden brown. When done, remove with a slotted spoon and place on kitchen paper to drain. Serve while still hot, sprinkled with sea salt.

SMOKED SALMON & GOAT'S CHEESE TARTLETS

BLOODY MARY SCALLOP CEVICHE

SMOKED SALMON & GOAT'S CHEESE TARTLETS

Serves 6 as an hors d'oeuvre

- 125g mild, creamy goat's cheese
- 1 tsp each dill, mint, parsley and chives, finely chopped
- 125g smoked salmon
- 1 packet of ready-made mini tartlet cases (see note)
- Dill fronds, to serve

1 Mash the goat's cheese with a fork and add the herbs, then season to taste with sea salt and black pepper. Lay out the smoked salmon slices on a board and divide the goat's cheese mixture between them. Spread the cheese evenly on the salmon slices before rolling them up. Cut the salmon rolls into pieces big enough to fit into the pastry cases. Serve garnished with dill fronds.
Note Mini tartlet cases are available at Sainsbury's and other large supermarkets in the specialist cooks ingredients section.

BLOODY MARY SCALLOP CEVICHE

Serves 6

- 20ml vodka
- 150ml chilled tomato juice
- Juice of 1 lime
- 3 dashes of worcestershire sauce
- 2 dashes of Tabasco
- A pinch of celery salt
- Olive oil
- 12 very fresh small scallops on the shell
- Chopped coriander leaves and lime wedges, to serve

1 Mix together the vodka, tomato juice, worcestershire, Tabasco and celery salt. Pour over each scallop, then drizzle with olive oil and scatter with coriander. Serve immediately with lime wedges.

HADDOCK PATE

HADDOCK PATE
Serves 6
- 570g smoked haddock
- 2 fresh bay leaves
- 1 litre milk
- 140ml double cream
- Juice and zest of 1 lemon
- 75g melted butter, plus more to pour over top
- 1 tbsp horseradish sauce
- ½ tbsp worcestershire sauce
- ½ tsp ground white pepper
- ½ tsp cayenne

1 Place haddock and bay leaves in a saucepan, cover with milk, adding extra cold water if necessary, so the haddock is just covered. Bring to boil over medium heat, then simmer over low heat for 10-15 minutes. Drain in a colander then place haddock in a bowl. Remove skin and any bones from haddock, then allow haddock pieces to cool. Transfer to food processor with cream, lemon juice and zest, melted butter, horseradish, worcestershire sauce, white pepper and cayenne. Season with sea salt and blend to a coarse paste. Transfer to a bowl and pour over enough extra melted butter to cover the mixture. Refrigerate overnight then serve with toast.

Super sandwiches

For almost any occasion, it's hard to beat the humble sarnie. Classic high tea or cocktail sandwiches (see right) can also be made with egg and cress, tiny shrimp and mayo, or paper-thin slices of cucumber. More substantial are classic New Orleans bites like the muffaletta and oyster po' boy, made by filling a baguette with lightly-battered fried shrimp or oysters, lettuce, tomato and mayo. For a muffaletta, halve a round loaf, remove some of the bread and cover the base with pickled vegetables and peppers. Add mortadella, salami, prosciutto, swiss and provolone cheeses and more pickled veg. Brush the top half of the bread generously with olive oil and place on top. Allow to marinate for 30 minutes, then serve hot (warmed in an oven till the cheese melts) or cold in slices. Smoked salmon with dill mayo on rye is a classic open sandwich and for a late-night snack you can't beat grilled cheddar on toast, spiced up with a splash of Tabasco or worcestershire sauce.

COCKTAIL SANDWICHES
Serves 6
- 2 cooked chicken breasts, shredded
- 2 celery sticks, very finely chopped
- 5 tbsp mayonnaise
- Juice of ½ lemon
- 10 slices thick-cut white bread
- Butter

1 Mix the chicken and celery with the mayo and lemon juice, then season with salt and pepper to taste. Butter your bread, make sandwiches using the chicken-mayo mixture, then carefully cut off the crusts. Slice each sandwich into 3 fingers, and serve as an early evening snack with a gin and tonic.

JAPANESE-STYLE PANCAKES

POLENTA CHIPS

JAPANESE-STYLE PANCAKES

Makes 10

- Olive oil
- 4 eggs, beaten
- 80g grated cheddar
- 100g shredded ham
- 3 tbsp mixed chopped fresh herbs, such as parsley, chives and basil
- 1 tbsp finely chopped chives
- Tomato ketchup, to serve

1 Put a frying pan over a medium heat with a little olive oil, then add a thin layer of beaten egg. When it's beginning to set, add the cheese, ham and fresh herbs. Remove from the pan, roll up and repeat with the remaining ingredients. Sprinkle with the chives and serve with a little bowl of ketchup for dipping.

POLENTA CHIPS

Recipe from Jamie's Italian
Serves 6

- 2 litres vegetable stock
- 300g polenta meal
- 30ml olive oil
- 50g grated parmesan, plus extra to serve
- Vegetable oil, for frying
- 1 sprig of rosemary, leaves picked

Rosemary salt

- 2 sprigs of rosemary, leaves picked
- 50g sea salt

1 To make the rosemary salt, using a pestle and mortar, bash the rosemary leaves with 1 teaspoon of salt to release the herb's oils. Combine with the remaining salt.
2 In a saucepan, boil the stock, then add the polenta and cook for 10-15 minutes,

stirring continuously so it stays smooth. When the stock is incorporated and the polenta is cooked, remove it from the heat and stir in the olive oil and parmesan, then season to taste with sea salt and freshly ground black pepper. Pour the polenta into a 30cm x 20cm tray and leave to cool, then place in the fridge until it's quite firm.
3 Heat vegetable oil, about 1cm deep, in a frying pan over a hot heat. Cut the polenta in 2-3cm squares. Very carefully, fry the polenta squares in batches until they're light golden. Add some rosemary leaves, then continue to cook the polenta chips until they're dark golden. Using a slotted spoon, place chips on kitchen paper to drain. Season with rosemary salt and serve immediately, sprinkled with a little extra parmesan and some of the fried rosemary leaves.

MOZZARELLA & PROSCIUTTO SANDWICHES

flour, then place on a tray until you're ready to cook them.

2 Place enough olive oil to come about 1.5cm up the sides of a large frying pan. (Never leave hot fat unattended.) Place the pan over medium heat and when hot enough to fry the croquettes, carefully drop them into the pan and cook, turning, for about 5 minutes until golden brown. Drain on kitchen paper and continue frying the remaining croquettes in batches until they're all cooked. Serve immediately.

CROCHETTE DI CACIOCAVALLO

Recipe from Nicolo Ravida
Serves 4

- 195g plain flour
- 200g fine breadcrumbs
- 500g boiled potatoes, mashed
- 400g caciocavallo or pecorino cheese
- 3 tbsp grated parmesan
- 2 eggs, beaten
- 600ml olive oil, for frying

1 Place the flour and 300ml cold water in a bowl, and whisk until well combined. Place breadcrumbs on a large plate.
2 Combine the potatoes, cheeses and eggs in a bowl. Season with freshly ground black pepper and a little salt. Make walnut-sized balls in ball of your hand. Dip in the croquettes in the flour and water mix then roll in breadcrumbs.
3 Pour enough olive oil into a large frying pan to come about 1.5cm up the sides. (Never leave hot fat unattended.) Heat over medium heat and, when the oil is hot, carefully fry the croquettes in batches, turning as they cook, for about 5 minutes, until golden brown. Drain on kitchen paper and continue cooking in batches until all croquettes are cooked. Serve immediately.

MOZZARELLA & PROSCIUTTO SANDWICHES

Serves 2

- 1 egg
- 3 tbsp milk
- 4 slices rustic, ciabatta-style bread
- 1 large fresh mozzarella, sliced
- 4 slices prosciutto
- Olive oil and butter, for frying

1 Whisk up the egg and milk and season. Top 2 bread slices with mozzarella and prosciutto and season. Cover with remaining bread, then dip and turn the sandwiches in the egg mixture. Fry in a pan with oil and butter over medium heat for 5 minutes each side, till golden and the mozzarella begins to melt.

RICOTTA CROCHETTE

Recipe from Nicolo Ravida
Serves 4

- Plain flour, for dusting
- 300g drained ricotta
- 3 tbsp grated pecorino cheese
- 1 tbsp finely chopped flat-leaf parsley
- 60g fine breadcrumbs
- 600ml olive oil, for frying

1 Place the flour on a plate. Combine the ricotta, pecorino, parsley and breadcrumbs in a bowl. Season with freshly ground black pepper and a little sea salt to taste. Take a heaped tablespoon of the ricotta mixture and make a round flattened croquette in your hand. Dust the croquettes in

RICOTTA CROCHETTE;
CROCHETTE DO CACIOCAVALLO

EASY SAMOSAS

Pastries

Frozen sheets of filo pastry are useful for making small triangle or cigar-shaped pies. Fill them with anything you fancy: combine tinned tuna with harissa, tomato passata and capers; make a classic Greek spinach or feta filling; or try a Turkish-style combo of rice, tomato, pine nuts and currants. Use leftover roast lamb or chicken, curry or stew – even leftover veg such as squash or peas, mashed with fresh herbs and a little butter. Pan fry or bake filo pastries (brushing tops with olive oil or melted butter) before serving with pesto, tomato and chilli salsa or yoghurt dips. For a sweet snack, make filo parcels with stewed apple, or ricotta sweetened with a little icing sugar and flavoured with grated lemon zest or dark chocolate.

BEEF CIGARS

EASY SAMOSAS

Makes 16

- 3 cooked medium potatoes
- 2 tbsp ready-made tandoori paste
- 3 spring onions, chopped
- 2 handfuls of frozen peas
- 1 packet of spring roll pastry
- 300ml vegetable oil

1 Put potatoes in a bowl and mash with tandoori paste, spring onions and peas. Season to taste with salt and pepper. One sheet of pastry at a time, add a little filling to each, then shape into triangles, using water to seal edges.
2 In a saucepan or very large frying pan, heat the oil until a cube of bread crisps in 30 seconds. Very carefully, fry the samosas in batches. When they're golden, remove with a slotted spoon and drain on kitchen paper before serving.

BEEF CIGARS & HARISSA SAUCE

Makes 15

- 3 tbsp olive oil
- 500g beef mince
- 1 tsp each dried mint and dried oregano
- 2 tbsp finely chopped parsley
- 2 garlic cloves, finely chopped
- 1 onion, grated
- 1 carrot, grated
- 1 celery stick, finely chopped
- 1 tsp harissa
- 1 tbsp tomato purée
- 1–2 tbsp tomato passata
- 1 packet of filo pastry
- Melted butter, for brushing

Harissa sauce
- 150g Greek-style thick yoghurt
- 1 tbsp harissa
- Juice of 1 lemon

1 Heat olive oil in a frying pan over a medium heat and sauté mince until browned. Add herbs, garlic, onion, carrot and celery, and cook for 5 minutes. Season to taste. Add harissa, tomato purée and passata. Turn down heat to low and cook for 30 minutes, then remove from heat and allow to cool.
2 Preheat the oven to 180C/gas 4. Lay out the filo sheets lengthways away from you, then cut them in half. Brush the edges of a pastry strip with melted butter, then place some filling across the bottom and roll up into a cigar, tucking in the edges. Repeat until you've used up all the filling, working quickly so the pastry doesn't dry out. Brush the cigars with butter, lay on baking tray and cook for 15–20 minutes.
3 Meanwhile, combine yoghurt, harissa and lemon juice to make a sauce, then serve with the hot beef cigars.

POTSTICKERS

POTSTICKERS

Recipe by Hui Mei Yang

Makes about 100 dumplings

- 1.2kg flour
- Vegetable oil
- Soy sauce, sesame oil and minced spring onion, to serve

Filling

- 1.2kg pork mince
- 7.5cm piece of ginger, grated
- 8 spring onions, minced
- Half a head of napa or Chinese white cabbage, finely shredded
- 4 tbsp soy sauce
- 3 tbsp sesame oil
- 1 tsp sugar

1 Put the flour in a bowl and make a well in the centre. Add 475ml water and mix thoroughly. Turn out onto a clean surface and knead for 10 minutes, till smooth, elastic and no longer sticks to your hands (or mix for 2–3 minutes in a stand mixer with the dough hook). Wrap dough in clingfilm and allow to rest for 30 minutes.
2 Combine filling ingredients in a large bowl and mix thoroughly with your hands. Fry a teaspoon of the mixture in oil in a hot pan until brown, taste for seasoning and adjust as necessary.
3 Pull off a handful of wrapper dough and roll into a 2.5cm-diameter snake. Pull off a 2.5cm piece and shape into a ball. Flatten and roll out about 1mm thick (nearly translucent) and 5cm in diameter. Keep dough and wrappers covered with clingfilm while you work to prevent them from drying out.
4 Place about 2 teaspoons of filling into the centre of a wrapper and fold dough in half. Starting at one end, take the sides, fold towards the end and press together to form pleats. To avoid splitting, be sure not to overfill or leave any openings. Place on a well-floured surface, sprinkle with a little extra flour to keep from sticking together, and cover with clingfilm.
5 When you're ready to cook, heat 2 tablespoons of vegetable oil in a large non-stick frying pan over medium-high heat. Place as many dumplings in the pan as will fit, pleats facing up. Sprinkle flour in between the dumplings and allow dumplings to brown for about 5 minutes. Add 120ml water, cover pan, reduce heat to medium and cook for 10 minutes. Uncover and cook for 2–3 minutes to evaporate any liquid.
6 Serve dumplings golden-side up with a dipping sauce made from soy sauce, sesame oil and minced spring onion, to taste. Rice or black vinegars, chilli sauce, sliced chillies or crushed garlic are also possible additions to a dipping sauce.
Note Dumplings freeze well. Arrange uncooked dumplings on a tray so they aren't touching and place in freezer for 20 minutes. Transfer to a freezer bag and keep for up to two months.

PICKLED QUAIL EGGS

PICKLED QUAIL EGGS

- 60ml dry white wine
- ¼ tsp celery seeds
- ¼ tsp aniseed
- 8 cloves
- 2 bay leaves
- ½ tsp each fennel seeds, peppercorns and coriander seeds
- ½ tsp paprika
- ½ tsp sea salt
- 2 shallots, sliced
- 24 boiled and peeled quail eggs

1 Combine all the ingredients except the eggs in saucepan over a medium heat. Boil, then simmer for 2–3 minutes, then remove from heat and let cool. Place the eggs in a sterilised jar and then pour over the vinegar mix. Refrigerate and allow to marinate for at least 24 hours before eating.

PISTACHIO & ROSE COOKIES

Biscuits

To make a basic cookie dough, beat 125g butter with 100g caster sugar until light, then beat in 1 tsp vanilla extract and 1 beaten egg. Fold in 125g plain flour and a pinch of salt. Spoon the dough onto a piece of clingfilm, roll up and chill for half an hour or freeze until needed. Preheat the oven to 170C/gas 3. Slice rounds from the dough and bake for 8-12 minutes, till done to your liking. You can stir in different chopped ingredients after adding the flour. Try dates and orange zest; cinnamon, sultanas and walnuts; white chocolate and dried cranberries; currants; almonds and dried apricots; or chocolate chips.

PISTACHIO & ROSE COOKIES

Makes 12
- 100g self-raising flour
- 50g butter
- 50g light brown sugar
- 1 tbsp golden syrup
- 2 tbsp rosewater
- 50g pistachios, finely ground in a blender or pestle and mortar

1 Preheat oven to 180C/gas 4. Add self-raising flour to a bowl with the butter, then rub together till the mixture resembles breadcrumbs. Add the sugar, golden syrup, rosewater and ground pistachios, then mix to combine. Divide dough into 12 pieces, flatten slightly and arrange on a baking tray, spaced apart to allow them to spread. Bake for 12 minutes, or until cookies are golden. Cool a little, then serve while still warm with a glass of lemon tea.

CHOCOLATE CHIP SODA BREAD

- 450g plain flour
- 1 tsp baking soda
- 1 tsp salt
- 1 tbsp caster sugar
- 100g dark chocolate, chopped
- 350ml buttermilk

1 Preheat the oven to 220C/gas 7. Mix the flour, baking soda, salt, sugar and chocolate in a large bowl. Make a well in the mixture and pour in the buttermilk. Mix the dough with one hand, fingers open, moving in a circle. Add more buttermilk if needed (the dough should be soft but not too wet). Put the dough on a baking sheet dusted with flour and shape into a 5cm-high round. Cut a cross in the top. Cook for 10 minutes, then turn the oven down to 200C/gas 6 for 30 minutes or until the bread is cooked. Remove from the oven, let it stand, then slice and serve while still warm.

CHOCOLATE CHIP SODA BREAD

Our wine match

La Croix du Chene is a classic red Rhône wine and a mean match for wild mushroom soup. Go to page 170 for more details of our great wine club offer.

SOUPS

QUICK SNACKS AND HEARTY MEALS – WAYS WITH BOILING WATER

It takes less than 15 minutes to prepare a saffron and pasta broth (page 28) or beetroot soup with spicy seeds (page 36). Cauliflower and stilton soup (page 35) offers simple comfort and Adam Perry Lang's short rib soup (page 32), though it requires a bit more effort, takes the chill off a winter's night

HOCK BROTH AND PEA &
MUSTARD DUMPLINGS

PUY LENTIL SOUP

HOCK BROTH AND PEA & MUSTARD DUMPLINGS

Serves 6-8

- 2kg smoked ham hock
- 1 sprig of bay leaves
- 5 black peppercorns
- 2 medium onions, roughly chopped
- 4 medium carrots, roughly chopped
- 4 sticks celery, roughly chopped, half the leaves reserved
- 100g plain flour
- 50g suet
- 1 pinch baking powder
- 1 tsp mustard powder
- Freshly grated nutmeg
- 2 small handfuls frozen peas
- Olive oil

1 You can do this step the day before. Soak the hock in water for 2 hours to remove excess salt. Put in a deep pot, cover with cold water and bay leaves, peppercorns and half each of the onion, carrot and celery. Bring slowly to the boil, reduce heat and simmer for 2¼ hours, skimming as needed.
2 When cooked, remove the hock, reserve and allow to cool slightly. Strain the stock and reserve. Discard the veg. Pull the meat apart using two forks and

reserve. Finely chop a few spoonfuls of ham and reserve for the dumplings.
3 For dumplings, mix the flour, suet, baking powder, mustard powder and a little nutmeg with your fingertips, then add the chopped ham and half the peas. Season and add cold water to bind. Dust your hands with flour and roll the mixture into brussels sprout-sized balls. Makes 16–18 dumplings.
4 Preheat the oven to 200C/gas 6. In a large ovenproof saucepan or casserole with a cover, heat 2 lugs of olive oil over a medium heat. Add the remaining onion, carrot and celery and sweat until soft. Add the ham and pour over 2.5 litres of the reserved stock. Drop in the dumplings and poke down under the surface. Cover and bake for 20 minutes or until the dumplings have soaked up some liquid and are fluffy. Add the remaining peas, cook for 2 minutes, sprinkle with celery leaves, then serve.

PUY LENTIL SOUP

Serves 4-6

- Olive oil
- 2 onions, finely chopped
- 3 garlic cloves, finely chopped
- 100g cubed pancetta
- 150g puy lentils

- Small bunch of thyme, leaves picked
- 200g butternut squash, diced
- 900ml chicken or vegetable stock
- 400g spinach
- 1 orange, for squeezing

1 Heat some olive oil in a large saucepan over a medium heat and add the onions, garlic and pancetta. Cook for 5 minutes, till lightly coloured, then add the lentils, thyme, butternut squash and stock. Simmer for 20 minutes, or until lentils are cooked through and tender. Add the spinach and cook for a couple of minutes until it wilts. Season the soup with salt and black pepper and finish with a squeeze of orange juice.

SAFFRON PASTA SOUP

Serves 1 hungry person

- 75g small soup pasta
- ½ tsp saffron threads
- 2 shallots, sliced
- 500ml stock
- Parmesan and chopped flat-leaf parsley, to serve

1 Put the pasta, saffron, shallots and stock into a saucepan and simmer till the pasta is cooked. Serve scattered with parmesan and parsley.

THAI CHICKEN NOODLE SOUP

CHICKEN & COCONUT SOUP

Serves 2-3

- 2 stalks lemongrass, chopped in half
- 4cm-piece ginger, peeled and chopped
- 4 garlic cloves, peeled
- 2 long red chillies, roughly chopped
- ½ tbsp shrimp paste
- 750ml coconut milk
- 6 kaffir lime leaves
- 200g skinless chicken breast, thinly sliced
- Juice of ½ lime
- 1 tbp fish sauce
- 12 baby corn
- 60g enoki mushrooms, trimmed
- 2 tbsp shaved palm sugar

1 Place lemongrass, ginger and garlic in a mortar and briefly pound with a pestle. Place this paste in a saucepan with the chillies, kaffir lime leaves, shrimp paste and coconut milk. Add about 50ml cold water, bring to the boil then simmer over low heat for 10-15 minutes. Take off heat and cool so that ingredients infuse the soup stock, before straining into a large bowl, discarding the solids.
2 Meanwhile, fill a small saucepan with water and bring to the boil. Lower the heat, add chicken pieces and simmer for 5 minutes until just cooked through. Strain, reserving the chicken.
3 Heat vegetable oil in a frying pan over medium heat, add shallots and sauté for 2 minutes before adding peanuts. Add chilli and cook for another minute before transferring fried mixture to a plate.
4 Meanwhile, pour infused stock back into saucepan, add chicken and corn to soup and simmer over low heat for 5 minutes, or until corn is cooked. Add enoki mushrooms, then season with fish sauce and lime juice before ladling into bowls. Add chopped ginger and fried peanuts, shallots and chilli to each bowl and serve immediately.

THAI CHICKEN NOODLE SOUP

Serves 2

- 600ml chicken stock
- 2 skinless chicken breasts, sliced
- 2 large shallots, thinly sliced
- Large piece of galangal, julienned
- 2 green chillies, sliced
- 200g rice vermicelli
- 4 small heads pak choi, sliced in half
- Handful of mangetout
- Coriander leaves, thai basil and sliced red and green chillies, to serve

1 Add the chicken stock to a saucepan and bring to the boil. Add the chicken slices, shallots, galangal and green chillies, then lower the heat and let the soup simmer for about 8 minutes, or until the chicken is cooked.
2 Add the rice vermicelli, pak choi and mangetout. Simmer for 2-3 minutes, until the noodles are cooked and the vegetables are tender. Ladle the soup, noodles and vegetables into bowls and sprinkle with some coriander and thai basil leaves and extra sliced fresh chillies, depending on how much heat you like. Serve immediately.

SHORT RIB SOUP

- 2 stalks of lemongrass
- 1 birds-eye (or milder) chilli
- 1 tbsp Japanese soy sauce
- 3 tbsp fish sauce
- 1 large white onion, chopped
- 1 large carrot, sliced
- 2.5cm-piece ginger, smashed
- Juice of 2 limes
- 5 cloves garlic, smashed
- Small bunch of fresh coriander
- 500g raw prawns, peeled, heads on
- 500g egg noodles, pre-blanched
- 10 baby carrots, peeled and split
- 10 baby corn, split
- 20 mangetout
- 2 bunches of enoki mushrooms, trimmed

Garnish
- 6 shallots, thinly sliced
- 1 bunch of spring onions, chopped
- 3 birds-eye chillies, thinly sliced
- Small bunch of fresh coriander
- 3 limes, for squeezing

1 For roast short rib, mix all ingredients and marinate, chilled, for at least 3 hours.
2 To make the broth, place the short rib, chicken and pork belly into a pot with stock and enough water to cover. Bring to the boil then reduce to a simmer, skimming any foam as required.
3 Meanwhile, preheat the oven to 140C/gas 1. Roast the marinated short rib for 3 hours, checking regularly.
4 After the broth has been cooking for 1 hour, remove the breast from the chicken and reserve. Add the star anise, kaffir lime leaves, lemongrass, chilli, soy sauce, fish sauce, onion, carrot pieces, ginger, lime juice, smashed garlic and fresh coriander. Continue to cook for 2 more hours. Keep spooning the fat off the surface while the soup is cooking.
5 When the soup has finished cooking, slice up the boiled meat – including the chicken breast – and the roasted short rib. Keep the meat slices warm in a low oven. Strain the broth and get rid of the carrot, onion and spices. Return broth to the pan, add the prawns, baby carrots, baby corn, mangetout and egg noodles, then cook for 4 minutes, or until the vegetables are tender and prawns are cooked. Serve the soup with the sliced meats and garnishes.

WATERCRESS SOUP

Serves 2-3
- Olive oil
- 2 potatoes, peeled and chopped
- 2 onions, chopped
- 2 garlic cloves, chopped
- 400ml stock
- 3 bunches of watercress, chopped

1 In a large saucepan, heat a little olive oil, then sauté the potatoes, onions and garlic until the onions are translucent. Add the stock and simmer until the potatoes are soft. Add the watercress and simmer for a further 3-4 minutes. Using hand blender, liquidise the soup until smooth, then serve with a swirl of crème fraîche and some Fortt's Bath Oliver biscuits.

SHORT RIB SOUP

Recipe by Adam Perry Lang
Serves 8
- 1kg short rib of beef, ask your butcher to cut it lengthways into 2 pieces

Roast short rib
- 1 piece short rib (as above)
- 1 tbsp fish sauce
- 1 tbsp soy sauce
- 3 garlic cloves, roughly chopped
- 1.5cm-piece fresh ginger
- 1 tsp chilli flakes
- 1 tbsp roasted sesame oil
- 1 tbsp vegetable oil

Broth
- 1 piece short rib (as above)
- 1 x 1.5kg chicken
- 500g piece pork belly
- 4 litres chicken stock
- 3 star anise
- 3 kaffir lime leaves

SOUPE DE 'CABBAGE'

Quick fixes

Combine soup pasta or rice with veg - try squash and broccoli; swede and carrot; or courgette and peas - cover with stock, simmer till tender, season and drizzle with olive oil. Sauté mushrooms with onion and garlic; add stock, simmer, blend and season. Roast onions and tomatoes, blitz with stock, simmer and serve with parmesan. Roast pumpkin, peppers and a few chillies, then blitz with stock and coconut milk. Simmer carrots, corn and greens in broth; season with soy and chilli. For a more substantial meal, add in some uncooked dumplings (page 23) and simmer until the dough is tender and filling cooked. For a super-fast soup, mix miso paste with boiling dashi stock or water, then add tofu and spring onion slices.

CAULIFLOWER & STILTON SOUP

CAULIFLOWER & STILTON SOUP

Serves 6

- 70g butter
- 1 onion, chopped
- 3 garlic cloves, sliced
- 1 tsp dried oregano
- 3 tbsp chopped parsley
- 1 cauliflower, chopped
- 1 litre vegetable stock
- 200g stilton, plus extra to serve
- 250ml milk

1 In a large pan, melt the butter, add the onion, garlic and oregano and sauté for 5 minutes, until onion is translucent. Add the parsley and cauliflower, then cook for 10 minutes. Add the vegetable stock; simmer for a further 20 minutes, until the cauliflower is tender.

2 Reserve a few cooked florets. Reduce the heat, add the stilton and milk, stir and cook for 5 minutes. Season, then purée with a hand blender until smooth. Reheat, garnish with the reserved cauliflower and extra stilton, then serve.

SOUPE DE 'CABBAGE'

Recipe by Stéphane Reynaud
Serves 6

- 1 firm savoy cabbage
- 3 fresh sorrel leaves, finely shredded
- 300g piece smoked streaky bacon, cut into 6 slices
- 100g butter, chopped

1 Remove 3 outer leaves from the cabbage, wash, finely shred and transfer to a bowl with the sorrel leaves. Cut away and discard any tough stalk from the base of the cabbage. Cut the rest of the cabbage finely and wash thoroughly. Place in a saucepan with the bacon, cover with water, bring to a boil, then simmer for 1 hour or until the bacon is tender. Drain in a fine colander, reserving the cooking liquid. Transfer the bacon to a plate and place the cooked cabbage in a food processor.
2 Add 80g butter to the cooked cabbage and mix well. Add about 1 litre of cooking liquid and blend well. Season with sea salt and ground black pepper.
3 Melt the remaining butter in a frying pan over a high heat and sauté the reserved cabbage leaves and sorrel for 2-3 minutes, then season to taste.
4 Pour the cabbage soup into bowls. Divide the reserved bacon slices and sautéed cabbage and sorrel between the bowls and serve immediately.

QUICK BEETROOT SOUP

Chop the beetroot and add to a blender with the onion, celery and stock. Blitz until smooth, adding the orange juice at the end. Season generously with salt and black pepper. Gently reheat, and serve with goat's cheese crumbled over and a scattering of chilli seeds.

PISTOU SOUP
Serves 4

- 4 tbsp olive oil
- 1 onion, chopped
- 3 leeks, sliced
- 3 garlic cloves, finely chopped
- 3 potatoes, chopped
- 3 carrots, chopped
- 2 fresh bay leaves
- 1 celery stick, chopped
- 1 tbsp chopped parsley
- 3 courgettes, chopped
- 250g baby green beans
- 1 x 400g can cannellini beans, drained
- 1 x 400g can borlotti beans, drained
- 1 x 400g can chopped tomatoes
- 70g small macaroni

Pistou sauce
- 5 garlic cloves
- Small handful fresh basil leaves
- 60g grated parmesan
- 3 tbsp olive oil

1 Heat the oil in large saucepan over a medium heat and sauté the onion, leeks and garlic for 5 minutes. Add all the other ingredients except the pasta, cover with water, season well and simmer till the vegetables are tender. Add the pasta and simmer till cooked, adding water if the soup is too thick.
2 For the pistou sauce, combine the garlic, basil and sea salt in a mortar and pound with pestle until puréed, add the parmesan and olive oil to make a paste. Serve the soup with a dollop of pistou.

Fassoulada

Something of a national dish, this is a simple Greek soup. Place 500g dried haricot beans (soaked overnight and drained) in a saucepan, cover with cold water and bring to boil, skimming off foam. Add 1 diced onion, 3 sliced carrots, 3 sliced celery sticks, 3 diced tomatoes, 2 tbsp tomato purée, 4 tbsp olive oil, 2 bay leaves and 3 tbsp chopped parsley and simmer gently for 2 hours till beans are tender. Season and serve.

QUICK BEETROOT SOUP
Serves 6

- 1 onion, chopped
- 2 celery sticks, chopped
- Olive oil
- 1.2kg precooked beetroot
- 700ml hot vegetable stock
- 50-100ml orange juice, to taste
- 100g goat's cheese

Chilli seeds
- 50g mixed seeds, such as pumpkin, sunflower and sesame
- 1 tsp chilli powder

1 To make the chilli seeds, dry fry the mixed seeds and chilli powder in a little frying pan for 2-3 minutes, stirring.
2 In a saucepan, soften the onion and celery in some olive oil over a low heat.

PARSNIP SOUP

CHICKEN & AVOCADO SOUP

Serves 4-6

- 2 skinless chicken breasts
- 2 skinless chicken thighs
- 4 spring onions , chopped
- 2 sprigs of coriander, chopped
- 3 bay leaves
- 20ml olive oil
- 2 corn cobs, sliced
- 8 new potatoes
- 1 sweet potato, chopped
- 1 chilli, sliced, plus extra to serve
- 2 avocados, sliced
- Capers and crème fraîche (optional), to serve

1 Put all the chicken, spring onions, coriander, bay, olive oil and salt in a pan. Cover with water. Bring to the boil, then simmer for 10 minutes. Add the corn, new and sweet potatoes and chilli, and season well. Cook for 15-20 minutes.
2 Slice the chicken, then transfer to bowls with the soup and avocado slices. Serve with extra chilli, capers and crème fraîche, if desired.

PARSNIP SOUP

Serves 4-6

- Olive oil
- 500g parsnips, trimmed and chopped
- 1 onion, diced
- 1 garlic clove, crushed
- 1½ tsp ground cumin
- 2½ tsp curry powder
- 1 litre vegetable stock
- 150ml double cream
- Sour cream, to serve

Parsnip crisps

- Vegetable oil
- 1 small parsnip, peeled into ribbons with a speed peeler

1 Heat a lug of oil in a saucepan and add the parsnips and onion. Cook, stirring, for 10-15 minutes, until softened. Stir in the garlic, cumin and curry powder, then cook for a further minute. Add the vegetable stock and simmer, uncovered, until the parsnip is cooked.
2 Meanwhile, to make the parsnip crisps fill a small pan a few inches deep with vegetable oil and put on a medium heat. Once the oil is hot, fry the parsnip strips in small batches until golden. Drain on kitchen paper and sprinkle with sea salt. Put to one side until needed.
3 Once the soup is cooked, add the cream and blitz with a hand blender until smooth. Season to taste with salt and black pepper. Reheat gently and serve with sour cream and scattered with a few of the parsnip crisps.

Our wine match

Arabella Chenin Blanc is a perfect counterpoint to a Greek horiatiki salad with fresh tomatoes, salty feta and dried oregano. Go to page 170 for more details of our wine offer.

SALAD & VEG

EAT YOUR GREENS... AND YOUR ORANGES, REDS AND YELLOWS

Simple doesn't mean boring when it comes to salads – grated carrot is lifted by cumin and orange (page 42), while tomatoes are transformed with a herby dressing (page 54). For something more substantial, try a warming leek gratin (page 58) or Antonio Carluccio's crunchy grilled polenta (page 50)

PETIT AIOLI

CAULIFLOWER VINAIGRETTE

PETIT AIOLI

Add meats, such as the pork loin on page 98, to turn this into a Grand Aïoli.
Serves 10–12

- 1kg baby potatoes, boiled
- 750g green beans, trimmed and boiled
- 12 carrots, trimmed and boiled
- 16 baby turnips, trimmed and boiled
- 24 shallots, peeled and boiled
- 12 asparagus spears, boiled
- 1kg beetroots, boiled, peeled and cut into eighths
- 12 baby leeks, trimmed and boiled
- 12 small artichokes, trimmed (choke removed, tops cut off and discarded), halved then boiled
- 3 fennel heads, trimmed and cut into wedges
- 2 bunches of radishes, trimmed
- 2 yellow peppers, deseeded and sliced
- 2 x 400g cans chickpeas, drained
- 12 eggs, boiled and halved
Aïoli
- 6 garlic cloves, sliced
- 1 tbsp sea salt
- 2 egg yolks
- 375ml extra-virgin olive oil
- Juice of ½ lemon

1 For aïoli, combine garlic and salt in a mortar and pound with pestle to a thick paste. Stir in egg yolks and combine well. Slowly add olive oil in a steady stream, stirring continuously with pestle, until the mixture emulsifies and thickens. Stir in lemon juice, cover with clingfilm and refrigerate until ready to use.
2 Place cooked and raw vegetables on various serving platters. Add chickpeas, eggs, baguettes and aïoli and serve immediately, with roast pork and/or chicken, if desired.

CAULIFLOWER VINAIGRETTE

Serves 4 as a side

- 8 baby cauliflowers
- 2 tsp capers
- 4 anchovy fillets, chopped
- 1 garlic clove, chopped
- 2 tbsp finely chopped flat-leaf parsley
- Juice of 1 lemon
- 60–80ml extra-virgin olive oil

1 Steam the baby cauliflowers for 2–3 minutes. Meanwhile, make a dressing with the remaining ingredients, then season to taste with freshly ground black pepper. Transfer the cauliflowers to a serving bowl, then drizzle with the dressing and gently toss to combine. Serve immediately.

CARROT & ORANGE SALAD

Serves 4

- 4 carrots, peeled and shredded
- Juice of 3 oranges
- 2 tsp ground cumin
- 60ml extra-virgin olive oil

1 Mix ingredients in a bowl, and season generously. Let everything marinate for 20 minutes before serving.

BEAN STEW;
COURGETTE FLOWERS

BEAN STEW

Use whatever fresh beans you can get.

Serves 4-6

- 6 tbsp extra-virgin olive oil
- 5 garlic cloves, sliced
- ½ head celery, sliced
- 7 baby leeks, sliced
- 4 banana shallots, sliced
- 400g carrots, sliced
- 4 fresh bay leaves
- ½ tbsp dried oregano
- ½ tbsp dried mint
- 720g runner beans, cut in half
- 750g borlotti beans, shelled
- 500g white haricot beans, shelled
- 4 plum tomatoes, roughly chopped
- 250g savoy cabbage, thinly sliced
- ½ bunch flat-leaf parsley, chopped

1 Heat the olive oil in a large saucepan over a medium heat and sauté the garlic, celery, leeks and shallots for 5 minutes, until softened. Add the carrots, bay leaves, oregano and mint and cook for a further 5 minutes. Add the beans, stir and cook for 5 minutes.
2 Add remaining ingredients, then pour in water to just cover the mixture. Season generously with sea salt and black pepper and stir. Bring to the boil, then lower the heat and simmer for 1½-2 hours or until the vegetables are tender and the sauce has thickened.
3 Allow the stew to cool, then serve lukewarm with toast. Or chill and serve the next day – it's even more delicious.

COURGETTE FLOWERS

Serves 4

- 12 courgettes, with flowers
- 3 tbsp extra-virgin olive oil
- 2 red onions, finely chopped
- 2 garlic cloves, finely chopped
- 135g long-grain rice
- 1 tsp sweet paprika
- 4 plum tomatoes, 2 finely chopped and 2 sliced
- 2 tbsp each fresh chervil, mint, parsley, basil, tarragon, chopped
- 1 lemon, cut into wedges

1 Carefully separate the flowers from the courgettes. Heat the oil in a frying pan over a medium heat and sauté the onions and garlic for 3-5 minutes, until softened. Add the rice and paprika and cook for a further 2-3 minutes. Add the chopped tomatoes, season with sea salt and black pepper, and cook for 5 minutes. Transfer to a bowl, add the herbs, mix well and allow to cool.
2 Stuff each flower with a heaped teaspoon of rice (don't overstuff as the rice expands during cooking). Fold the sides of each flower over the stuffing.
3 Put the sliced tomatoes in a large frying pan and drizzle with olive oil. Place the courgette flowers on top. Add 300ml water and cook over a medium heat, covered, for 25-35 minutes or until the tomatoes and courgette flowers are tender and the rice is cooked.
4 Meanwhile, steam or boil the remaining courgettes for 2-3 minutes or until just cooked. Drain, then slice and serve in a bowl with a little sea salt and a squeeze of lemon. Transfer the courgette flowers to a bowl and serve with the courgette slices.

CHICORY, DUCK & BEETROOT SALAD

CHICORY, DUCK & BEETROOT SALAD

Serves 1

- 1 medium head red chicory, half the leaves separated, remainder chopped
- 3 slices smoked duck
- 1 cooked beetroot, peeled and diced
- ½ bunch watercress
- ½ avocado, peeled and diced
- 3 tbsp extra-virgin olive oil
- 1 tbsp red wine vinegar

1 Combine ingredients in a salad bowl and season generously with sea salt and freshly ground black pepper.

BEST-EVER ROAST POTATOES & SALSA VERDE

paste. Loosen with a glug of oil and season carefully to taste. You can pulse the salsa verde a bit more so it's really fine and will cling to the roast potatoes, or you can keep it rustic.

4 Once your potatoes are golden, get a fish slice, or anything flat, and push down on them so their undersides are flat and better able to crisp up, and the sides burst open and are fluffy. Toss the rosemary in olive oil to coat, sprinkle over the potatoes and return to the oven for 10–15 minutes more.

5 Remove them once again and either finely slice the garlic with a knife or slice it on a mandolin, then sprinkle the slices over the potatoes to give you a top layer of perfectly thin and beautiful garlic slices. It will look insane and taste amazing. Drizzle over some more olive oil, then pop the potatoes back in the oven for 2 minutes until the garlic is golden and crisp. Season, then either present the potatoes in the tray or move them to a dish, and serve immediately with the salsa verde.

MATCHSTICK BEET SALAD

Serves 4 as a side

- 100g feta cheese
- Handful of fresh mint, flat-leaf parsley, fennel tops or dill, and green or purple basil
- 300g beets, washed and scrubbed
- 1 granny smith apple
- 1 fresh chilli (optional), finely sliced
- 8 tbsp extra-virgin olive oil
- 1 juicy lemon

1 Crumble the feta into a bowl. Finely slice your herbs and add them to the bowl, too. Thinly slice your beets and apple (core and all), then finely slice into matchsticks (or a food processor will do a fine job). Put these in the bowl along with your feta and herbs, then add the chilli, if using. Just before you serve it, pour on the olive oil, add the juice from your lemon and a good pinch of pepper. Toss everything together have a taste. The salt from the feta should be enough to season it but if not, add a pinch of salt, and toss again. Tuck in right away while it's fresh and crunchy.

BEST-EVER ROAST POTATOES & SALSA VERDE

Serves 6

- 1.5kg roasting potatoes
- Olive oil
- Knob of butter
- 6 sprigs of fresh rosemary
- 12 garlic cloves

Salsa verde

- 2–4 slices of ciabatta bread
- 2 tbsp good red wine vinegar
- ½ garlic clove, finely chopped
- Small bunch of mint, leaves picked
- Small bunch of flat-leaf parsley, leaves picked
- Few sprigs of thyme, leaves picked
- 4 anchovy fillets in oil
- 1 tbsp capers
- 1 tsp dijon mustard
- Extra-virgin olive oil

1 Preheat your oven to 220C/gas 7. Bring a large pan of salted water to the boil. Chop the potatoes into squash-ball sizes and parboil them for about 12–14 minutes, until they're almost cooked and soft around the edges.

2 Drain the potatoes and let them steam-dry for a minute, shaking them in the saucepan to scruff them up around the edges, so that they go really crispy when they're roasted. Pop the potatoes into a roasting tray in a single layer with a good pinch of salt and some pepper, a generous glug of olive oil and the knob of butter. Roast them for 30 minutes, or until they're golden brown.

3 Meanwhile, put the salsa verde ingredients, except for the oil, into a food processor and pulse to a chunky

GIGANTES PLAKI

Leftovers

Bubble and squeak is often made from leftovers. Smash up any veg from a Sunday dinner - potatoes, carrots, sprouts, peas - season well and then fry in hot butter and oil, or dripping, turning, so you get lots of lovely crunchy bits. You can mash cooked, cold squash or potatoes with butter and herbs, shape it into rounds (binding with a beaten egg if necessary) and fry. Eat for breakfast, or with leftover roast meat for lunch. For quick fishcakes, add a tin of tuna to leftover mashed potatoes and mix well, then stir in chopped spring onions, salt and pepper to taste, and fry until hot throughout. Leftover roast squash or beetroot is brilliant in salads with rocket, feta, toasted seeds and a simple dressing.

BUBBLE & SQUEAK

Serves 4 as part of a breakfast or mixed grill

- 1kg floury potatoes, peeled, quartered
- 1 large cabbage, cored and finely shredded
- Olive oil
- Large knob of butter
- 1 tbsp English mustard, plus extra French or English mustard, to serve
- Extra-virgin olive oil

1 Place the potatoes in a pan of salted water and bring to the boil. Cook for 15–20 minutes then add the shredded cabbage and cook for a further 3 minutes until cooked through. Drain and set aside to steam dry.

2 Heat olive oil and butter in a large frying pan then add the potatoes and cabbage. Mash them, season to taste, then pat into a pancake. Fry on medium heat for 15–20 minutes, checking every 5 minutes and flipping over bit by bit until lovely and crisp all over.

3 Slice the bubble and squeak into wedges, and serve with mustard, a drizzle of extra-virgin olive oil, with bacon and coffee for breakfast, or as part of a mixed grill.

GIGANTES PLAKI

Serves 4

- 500g dried butter beans, soaked overnight
- 3 tbsp extra-virgin olive oil
- 1 onion, finely chopped
- 2 garlic cloves, finely chopped
- 2 carrots, thinly sliced
- 2 large tomatoes, peeled, chopped
- 1 tbsp tomato purée, dissolved in 125ml warm water
- 2 fresh bay leaves
- 2 tbsp flat-leaf parsley, chopped

1 Drain beans, and place in a saucepan. Cover with cold water and bring to the boil, skimming off any foam. Simmer for 40 minutes, till most of the water has been absorbed. Drain and let cool.

2 Preheat oven to 180C/gas 4. Heat oil in a pan over medium heat, add onion and garlic and soften for 7 minutes. Add carrots, tomatoes, tomato purée, bay and parsley and simmer for 10 minutes. Combine with beans, season with salt and pepper and transfer to a casserole. Bake for 1–1½ hours, until beans are soft and browned, and most liquid has been absorbed. Serve lukewarm or cold with a drizzle of olive oil.

POLENTA CRUST & CHICORY

turn and repeat on the other side. It should take about 8 minutes each side to get a good crust (longer if you like a thick crust – it can almost be burnt). Serve polenta crusts with the leaves, plus a little of the cooking juices.

WILD MUSHROOM SALAD

Recipe by Gennaro Contaldo
Serves 4

- 300g closed-cap horse, mixed wild or chestnut mushrooms
- Juice of 2 large lemons
- 6 tbsp extra-virgin olive oil
- ¼ red chilli, finely chopped
- 2 garlic cloves, sliced
- Handful of flat-leaf parsley, finely chopped
- 10 large black or green olives, sliced
- Lemon wedges, to serve

1 Clean the mushrooms with a cloth and brush (generally, do not wash wild mushrooms as the flavour disappears). Roughly chop any large mushrooms and leave small ones intact. Put the lemon juice and some salt in a litre of water in a saucepan, bring to the boil and add the mushrooms. Simmer for about 4 minutes. Meanwhile, combine the oil, chilli, garlic, parsley and olives in a bowl. Drain the mushrooms and immediately add to the marinade. Mix well, check the seasoning, then leave to cool. Serve with lemon wedges.

POLENTA CRUST & CHICORY

Recipe by Antonio Carluccio
Serves 4

- 200g quick-cook polenta
- 2 tbsp olive oil, plus extra for frying

Braised chicory

- 600g chicory or curly kale, wild dandelion leaves, batavia, purple sprouting broccoli, cavolo nero or a mixture of any bitter leaves
- 6 tbsp olive oil
- ½ small red chilli, chopped
- 1 tbsp salted capers, soaked and drained
- 2 garlic cloves, chopped
- 1 chicken stock cube

1 To make the braised chicory, chop the leaves into large chunks. Put the olive oil, chilli, capers and garlic in a saucepan over a low heat and cook for about 3 minutes. Add the leaves, along with 300ml water, and crumble in the chicken stock cube. Cover with a lid, reduce the heat, and cook for 15–20 minutes, until the toughest stalks are tender. Check the seasoning and adjust as required . By this time, there should be lots of cooking juices. Turn off the heat and keep warm.
2 Meanwhile, put the quick-cook polenta in a bowl with the olive oil, season with sea salt and freshly ground black pepper and mix well. Add 150ml boiling water to make a dough. Divide into 6 pieces, and pat out to make cakes the size of thick hamburgers. Place a frying pan over a medium heat, add a little olive oil and cook the polenta cakes on one side until a crust has formed. Add a few more drops of oil,

HORIATIKI SALAD

STUFFED SQUASH

HORIATIKI SALAD

Serves 4

- 125g Greek feta, crumbled into chunks
- 2 green peppers, deseeded and sliced
- 1 cucumber, peeled and sliced
- Handful of kalamata olives
- 5 ripe tomatoes, sliced
- 1 small red onion, sliced
- 1 tsp dried oregano
- 3–4 tbsp extra-virgin olive oil
- 3–4 tbsp red wine vinegar
- Crusty bread, to serve

1 Combine all the ingredients except the oregano, oil and vinegar in a salad bowl. Just before serving, sprinkle the salad with the oregano, season with freshly ground black pepper and dress with the olive oil and vinegar. Serve this classic Greek salad with good bread.

STUFFED SQUASH

Serves 4

- 4 small squash
- Extra-virgin olive oil
- 6 rashers of pancetta
- 100g gruyère
- Handful of cooked, vacuum-packed chestnuts
- Small handful of sage leaves, roughly chopped
- Large chunk of ciabatta, torn into small pieces
- 1 egg, beaten

1 Preheat oven to 200C/gas 6. Slice the tops off of the squash. Scoop seeds from squash to make a decent-sized cavity. Put squash in a small roasting tin so they sit snugly, then drizzle with extra-virgin olive oil.
2 Slice the rashers of pancetta into 2cm pieces and fry until golden, then transfer to a bowl. Grate in some gruyère, crumble the chestnuts and add some sage. Add the ciabatta and beaten egg to the bowl, then mix to combine. Stuff mixture into squash cavities, piling up as much as you can on top. Finish with a little grated gruyère and some sage, then drizzle with olive oil. Roast for 30 minutes, or until the squash is cooked through. Transfer to plates and serve immediately.

END OF SEASON TOMATO SALAD

END OF SEASON TOMATO SALAD

Serves 4-6

- 800g mixed tomatoes, all colours, shapes and sizes
- 2 punnets of cress
- Large bunch of fresh basil, marjoram or oregano, or a mixture of the three, leaves picked
- Juice of ½ a lemon
- Good-quality red wine vinegar
- Extra-virgin olive oil
- Large handful of mixed leaves, such as mustard leaf, rocket or frisée, washed and spun dry
- 6 ready-to-eat poppadoms
- 150g feta cheese

1 Chop up your tomatoes, halving the smaller ones, and cutting any large ones into chunks. Put them in a bowl with good pinches of salt and pepper and leave to sit for 5-10 minutes.
2 Using a pestle, bash your fresh herbs up in a large mortar with salt and pepper until you get a wonderful herby paste. Add the lemon juice and a splash of red wine vinegar, then pour in three times as much extra-virgin olive oil and give everything a good mix.
3 Pour away any juice that has collected at the bottom of your bowl of tomatoes, drizzle over your herby dressing, then use your hands to toss your tomatoes.
4 Just before serving, toss the leaves in with the tomatoes, then break over the poppadoms and crumble in the feta.

BEETROOT WITH PURSLANE

In Greece, *glistrida* (purslane) is often collected wild and added to salads.

Serves 4

- 400g beetroot, including stems, boiled, then peeled and sliced
- 60g purslane or watercress
- 4 tbsp extra-virgin olive oil
- 2 tbsp white wine vinegar
- Crusty bread, to serve

1 Combine the beetroot and purslane in a bowl, and season with sea salt and freshly ground black pepper. Drizzle with the olive oil and white wine vinegar and eat with crusty bread.

BEETROOT WITH PURSLANE

STUFFED ARTICHOKES

Recipe from Nicolo Ravida
Serves 4-6

- 2 lemons, halved
- 12 small artichokes
- 3 tbsp breadcrumbs
- 3-4 tbsp grated pecorino or parmesan cheese
- 1 tsp grated lemon zest
- 1 tbsp finely chopped flat-leaf parsley
- 1 garlic clove, grated
- 4 tbsp extra-virgin olive oil

1 Squeeze the lemon halves into a bowl of cold water. Cut the woody ends off the artichoke stalks, discard, then peel any remaining stalk. Clean artichokes by removing tough outer leaves. Chop off the top half of the leaves and scrape out the choke from the centre. Place in the acidulated water.
2 Combine the breadcrumbs, cheese, lemon zest, parsley, garlic, half the olive oil and season generously with sea salt and ground black pepper.
3 Fill the artichokes with the bread mixture, then place in a large saucepan. Add cold water to come halfway up the sides of the artichokes, sprinkle with sea salt and drizzle with remaining olive oil. Cover, bring to boil over medium heat then simmer artichokes for about 15 minutes, till tender. Remove from pan, then serve lukewarm.

QUINOA & ROAST BEETROOT

QUINOA & ROAST BEETROOT

Recipe by Giovanni Esposito, Giovanni's Deliworld, Cape Town, South Africa

- 500g quinoa, washed
- 500g roasted beetroot (see right), diced finely
- 500g balsamic onions (see right), diced finely
- 100ml extra-virgin olive oil
- 2 tbsp chopped flat-leaf parsley
- 2 tbsp chopped chives

1 In a saucepan, add quinoa to 1 litre of cold water, bring to the boil and then simmer for 15 minutes or until just tender. Drain and cool down with cold water. Combine with remaining ingredients, season with sea salt and lots of freshly ground black pepper and serve sprinkled with chopped chives.

ROASTED BEETROOT

- 1kg medium-sized beetroot, skin on, quartered
- 50ml extra-virgin olive oil
- 80ml balsamic vinegar
- 2 bay leaves
- 10g sugar

1 Preheat oven to 200C/gas 6. Place beetroot in a roasting tray, season and combine with remaining ingredients, coating well. Cover with foil and roast for 30 minutes. Remove foil, stir and turn beetroot and cook uncovered for about an hour, until just tender. Use in salads or serve on lunch platters with cheese and pickles.

BALSAMIC ONIONS

- 1kg pearl onions, peeled
- 50ml extra-virgin olive oil
- 120ml balsamic vinegar
- 30g sugar

1 Preheat oven to 200C/gas 6. Place onions in a roasting tray, then cook as for roasted beetroot, until slightly caramelised. Use in salads or serve on platters with cured meats.

DHAL

Gratins

DHAL

Recipe by Deep Mohan Singh Arneja
Serves 4

- 250g small yellow lentils (mung dhal)
- 100g small orange lentils (mysoar dhal)
- ¾ tsp turmeric
- 3 tbsp ghee
- 1 tsp cumin seeds
- ½ medium onion, roughly chopped
- 1 dried red chilli
- 1 green chilli , deseeded and chopped
- ½ tsp Kashmiri chilli powder

1 Put the lentils in a bowl and cover with cold water. Rinse well, stirring, and when the water turns cloudy, change it and wash again till it remains clear.
2 Place the lentils in a saucepan with 1.75 litres water, boil, then reduce heat to a simmer. Skim any scum from the surface. Add the turmeric and a pinch of salt. Cook for 30 minutes, until soft.
3 Heat the ghee in a pan. Add the cumin seeds and, when they pop, add the onion and dried chilli. Stir, then cook until the onion is soft and lightly golden. Add the green chilli and chilli powder and give everything a good stir, tip over the warm dhal and serve with Indian breads.

LEEK GRATIN
Serves 4

- 12 parboiled leeks
- 500ml milk
- 2 bay leaves
- 60g butter
- 1 tbsp olive oil
- 60g flour
- ½ tsp ground nutmeg
- 100g parmesan, grated
- ½ cup breadcrumbs

1 Preheat oven to 180C/gas 4. Place the leeks in ovenproof dish. Heat milk and bay leaves in saucepan over low heat. Melt butter and olive oil in another saucepan over medium heat, add flour and stir continuously with wooden spoon for 5 minutes, till combined. Slowly ladle the milk into the flour mix, discarding bay leaves, and whisk till sauce thickens. Remove from heat, stir in the nutmeg and three-quarters of the cheese and pour over leeks. Combine the breadcrumbs and remaining parmesan and sprinkle over leeks. Bake for 40 minutes, till top is golden brown. Serve with roast chicken.

LEEK GRATIN

Our wine match

Milani Montepulciano d'Abruzzo with homemade pesto spaghetti is a magic combination. Go to page 170 for more information about our great wine club offer.

PASTA & RICE

Night owls can pair pasta with basics, like capers (page 62),
for a quick, late supper, and chilli fiends will find comfort in
arrabiata with a crunchy breadcrumb topping (page 70).
To impress dinner guests, try a champagne risotto (page 62),
or the prawn linguine (page 66) from Jamie's Italian

TOMATO & CAPER LINGUINE

SPINACH CANNELLONI

TOMATO & CAPER LINGUINE

Serves 4

- 400g linguine
- Olive oil
- 350g tomato passata
- 5 tbsp capers, rinsed
- Grated zest of ½ lemon
- Grated parmesan and extra grated lemon zest (optional), to serve

1 Bring a saucepan of salted water to the boil and cook linguine according to pack instructions.
2 Meanwhile, add a lug of olive oil to a medium saucepan on a medium heat. Add the tomato passata, capers and lemon zest and simmer for 5-7 minutes. Season to taste. When the linguine is al dente, drain and toss with the sauce to coat and then serve immediately, scattered with parmesan or extra lemon zest, if desired.

SPINACH CANNELLONI

Serves 4

- Olive oil
- 2 garlic cloves, chopped
- 600g baby spinach, chopped
- Grated zest of 1 lemon
- 300g ricotta
- 120g grated parmesan, plus extra for sprinkling
- 1 x 250g packet dried cannelloni
- 400-500ml béchamel sauce (see page 160)

1 Add a lug of olive oil to a medium-sized saucepan over a medium heat. Add the garlic and sauté until softened, then stir in the spinach. When wilted, transfer to a mixing bowl with the lemon zest, ricotta and parmesan. Mix to combine and season to taste with salt and black pepper.
2 Preheat your oven to 200C/gas 6. Using your hands, fill the cannelloni with the spinach-ricotta filling and then place them in an ovenproof dish so they fit tightly. Pour over the béchamel sauce, sprinkle with the extra parmesan and bake for 15-20 minutes, or until the cannelloni are tender. Remove from the oven and leave to stand for a few minutes before serving.

CHAMPAGNE & PRAWN RISOTTO

Serves 4

- Pinch of saffron
- Large knob of butter
- 1 onion, finely chopped
- 400g arborio rice
- 160ml champagne or dry sparkling white wine, plus extra to serve
- 1 litre chicken stock
- 300g cooked baby prawns, peeled

1 Place the saffron in a small bowl, cover with a splash of boiling water and leave to stand for a few minutes.
2 In a large saucepan over a medium heat, melt the butter and sauté the onion until soft. Add the rice and stir for a few minutes until it starts to go translucent. Add the champagne, stir and allow the alcohol to cook off. Stir in the saffron and its soaking water, then gradually add the stock a ladleful at a time, stirring in before adding the next. Once all the stock is added, keep stirring until the risotto is tender on the outside with a slight bite to the centre. Stir in the prawns and heat through before serving. Alternatively, heat the prawns in a separate pan and serve on top of the risotto. Add a dash of champagne to each plate for a decadent supper.

MUSHROOM & LEEK LASAGNE

Recipe by Dave Barker, Fox & Hounds,
Northamptonshire
Serves 6

- 2 tbsp olive oil
- Knob of butter
- 1 white onion, finely chopped
- 2 garlic cloves, finely chopped
- 4 leeks, thinly sliced
- 400g mushrooms
- 80g mixed dried wild mushrooms, soaked in 300ml water for at least 1 hour, then drained, mushrooms and water reserved separately
- 350g baby spinach, washed
- 500g dried lasagne sheets
- Baby mozzarella (optional), to top lasagne
- 40g grated parmesan, plus extra

Mushroom & parmesan béchamel

- 750ml semi-skimmed milk
- 250ml mushroom stock (soaking water, as above)
- 1 small onion, peeled but left whole
- 2 bay leaves
- 100g unsalted butter
- 70g plain flour
- 60g grated parmesan

1 For the béchamel, mix the milk and the reserved mushroom stock together in a large saucepan with the onion and bay leaves. Cook over a medium heat for 4 minutes, but do not let it boil. Meanwhile, in another pan on a low heat, melt the butter and then add the flour. Keep stirring the mixture for several minutes to cook the flour. This makes a roux. When the milk mixture is just coming to the boil, remove the onion and bay leaves with a slotted spoon. Whisk the roux into the milk and keep whisking over the heat until it thickens. Add the parmesan and season to taste with sea salt and freshly ground black pepper.

TOMATO ORZO

2 Preheat your oven to 180C/gas 4. Put a large frying pan on a medium heat and add the olive oil and butter. When they've melted together, add the onion, garlic, leek and fresh and rehydrated mushrooms and sauté for 5 minutes or so, stirring frequently. Add the spinach and continue stirring until it has wilted down. Season to taste, then add the mushroom béchamel to the vegetable mixture, and stir to combine.
3 Line the bottom of a 2-litre ovenproof dish with lasagne sheets. Spoon over half the vegetable mix. Top with a layer of lasagne sheets and then cover with remaining vegetable mixture. Top with torn mozzarella (if desired), sprinkle over the parmesan, then place in the oven to cook for 35–40 minutes, or until golden-brown and the lasagne is tender. Remove from oven, scatter with parmesan and serve with a green salad.

TOMATO ORZO

Serves 4 as a side

- Olive oil
- 2 onions, sliced
- 2 garlic cloves, sliced
- 250g orzo
- 1 tbsp chopped fresh marjoram
- 5 plum tomatoes, chopped
- Shaved parmesan (optional)

1 Add a lug of olive oil to a medium saucepan over a medium heat and sauté the onion and garlic until soft. Stir in the orzo and majoram and cook for 3 minutes, then stir in the tomatoes, seasoning to taste. Add water to cover the orzo, bring up to a simmer and cook, stirring occasionally, for 15 minutes or until tender. Transfer to a serving dish, scatter with parmesan if desired, and serve with grilled meat or fish.

PRAWN LINGUINE

VEAL MILANESE & SPAGHETTI POMODORO

Serves 4

- 100g breadcrumbs
- Grated zest of 1 lemon
- 40g grated parmesan
- 2 tbsp plain flour
- 2 eggs, beaten
- 4 x 120g veal escalopes
- 300g spaghetti
- Olive oil, for frying
- Grated parmesan (optional), to serve

Pomodoro sauce

- 3 tbsp olive oil
- 1 medium red onion, finely chopped
- 2 garlic cloves, finely chopped
- 2 x 400g tins tomatoes
- ½ tsp sugar
- Small bunch of basil, leaves picked and torn

1 Combine the breadcrumbs, zest and parmesan and season with salt and pepper. Put the flour on a plate, the breadcrumbs mixture on another and the eggs in a bowl. Dip each escalope, into the flour, then into the egg and lastly the breadcrumbs. Place them on a tray or plate and chill before cooking.
2 To make the pomodoro sauce, heat the olive oil in a saucepan over a low heat and gently cook the onions for 10 minutes until translucent. Add the garlic and cook, stirring, for a further 2 minutes. Add the tomatoes and sugar, then bring up to the boil. Stirring occasionally, allow the sauce to simmer gently for about 45 minutes, or until well reduced but not dry. As the sauce cooks, break up the tomatoes with a wooden spoon. Once cooked, season to taste and add the basil leaves.
3 Bring a large pan of salted water to the boil, add the spaghetti and cook according to packet instructions. Once it's al dente, drain and add to the sauce.
4 Meanwhile, in a frying pan over a medium heat, heat olive oil until sizzling and then add the escalopes. Cook in batches for 3-4 minutes each side, until golden-brown. Drain on kitchen paper and serve with the spaghetti and a little parmesan for the pasta, if desired.

PRAWN LINGUINE

Recipe from Jamie's Italian
Serves 2

- 200g linguine, fresh or dried
- Olive oil
- 1 tsp capers
- 6 anchovy fillets
- 4 garlic cloves, sliced
- 12 prawns, peeled, shells reserved
- 50ml white wine
- 1 medium onion, diced
- 1 tbsp tomato purée
- 350ml fish stock
- 1 tsp finely sliced fresh red chilli
- 6 cherry tomatoes, quartered
- 40g rocket
- 1 tsp finely chopped flat-leaf parsley
- Extra-virgin olive oil

1 Bring a large pan of salted water to the boil and cook linguine until al dente.

2 Meanwhile, add some olive oil to a heavy-based frying pan over a low heat and sweat the capers, anchovies and half the garlic for 2-3 minutes. Add the prawn shells and fry for 2-3 minutes. Add the wine and cook till reduced by half, then add the onion and tomato purée and cook till soft and starting to colour. Add the stock, bring to a simmer and cook for 5 minutes. Remove from heat, pour into a food processor and blend till smooth. Pass through a sieve and set aside.
3 In another frying pan, add some olive oil and fry chilli and remaining garlic till softened. Add the prawns and cook for 1-2 minutes. Add the prawn sauce, bring to a simmer and add the tomatoes, half the rocket and the parsley. Add the linguine, mix well and serve topped with remaining rocket and drizzled with extra-virgin olive oil.

VEAL MILANESE & SPAGHETTI POMODORO

COURGETTE CARBONARA

Recipe from Jamie's Italian

Serves 2

- 2 large eggs
- 30ml crème fraîche
- 25g finely grated parmesan
- 2 tsp olive oil
- 60g smoked pancetta, cubed
- ¼ red onion, sliced
- ½ yellow courgette, julienned
- ½ green courgette, julienned
- Grated zest of 1 lemon
- Baby or chopped herbs, to serve

Pasta

- 150g Italian '00' flour
- 50g semolina
- 2 medium free-range eggs

1 To make the pasta, mix the flour and semolina in a large bowl. Make a well and break in the eggs. Combine with a fork, then knead the dough for 5 minutes. Shape into a ball, wrap in clingfilm and refrigerate for 30 minutes. When you're ready, put the dough through a pasta-maker. If you don't have one, simply roll the dough into sheets about 2mm thick, then cut into thin strips.
2 In a bowl, beat the eggs with the crème fraîche, most of the parmesan and a grind of black pepper. Heat the olive oil in a heavy-based frying pan and fry the pancetta until crisp. Add the onion and fry for a further 2 minutes.
3 Boil a large pan of salted water and cook pasta for 3 minutes, or till al dente. Meanwhile, add the courgettes to the pancetta and onion and allow them to wilt. When the pasta is cooked, drain it, reserving a little water, and add both to the pan with the courgettes, tossing to combine. Remove from the heat and pour over the egg mixture. Gently combine, allowing the sauce to thicken. Serve immediately, scattered with the remaining parmesan, lemon zest and some baby or chopped herbs.

SPINACH & LEMON LINGUINE

SPINACH & LEMON LINGUINE

Serves 4

- 400g linguine
- 6 tbsp olive oil
- 50g fresh breadcrumbs
- Grated zest and juice of 1 lemon
- 3 garlic cloves, sliced
- 1 large red chilli (optional), chopped
- 600g baby spinach leaves, washed
- Grated parmesan (optional), to serve

1 Boil a pan of salted water, add the linguine and cook according to packet instructions. Meanwhile, in a large frying pan, heat 2 tablespoons of olive oil and fry the breadcrumbs for a couple of minutes until golden. Transfer to kitchen paper to drain, then mix with the lemon zest and set aside.
2 Heat the remaining oil in the pan, add the garlic and chilli and cook, stirring, for a couple minutes until the garlic begins to turn golden. Add the spinach and cook until it has wilted, seasoning with salt and black pepper to taste.
3 When the pasta is al dente, drain, reserving a little of the cooking water, and add to the pan with the spinach. Stir in the lemon juice, adding a little of the reserved cooking water to loosen as necessary. Lastly, sprinkle over the breadcrumb and lemon zest mixture, then serve, with parmesan, if desired.

DOUBLE WHAMMY ARRABIATA

ORECCHIETTE & LAMB RAGU

Serves 4-6

- 2kg shoulder of lamb
- Small bunch of fresh rosemary, plus 2 sprigs extra
- Olive oil, plus extra-virgin olive oil for drizzling
- 1 large onion, finely chopped
- 2 carrots, finely chopped
- 1 leek, finely chopped
- 2 celery stalks, finely chopped
- 4 garlic cloves, finely chopped
- 1 fresh bay leaf
- 2 sprigs fresh thyme
- ½ bottle red wine
- 300ml lamb stock, plus a bit extra
- 2 x 400g tins chopped tomatoes
- 400g dry orecchiette
- Fresh oregano leaves and parmesan cheese, to serve

1 Turn your oven up to full. Slash the fat side of the lamb all over. Scatter half the bunch of rosemary in a high-sided roasting tray, rub the lamb with oil, salt and black pepper. Place in the tray, and cover with remaining rosemary. Tightly cover with foil and place in the oven. Turn the oven down to 170°C/gas 3 and cook for 4 hours, until lamb pulls apart easily.
2 When cooked, place lamb on a board. Cover with a tea towel and rest until cool, then gently shred using two forks.
3 Add the vegetables and garlic to a large pan with the oil, bay leaf, thyme and extra rosemary. Cook for 15 minutes or until veg are soft. Pour in the wine and cook until most of it has evaporated. Add stock and tomatoes and cook gently for an hour. Season to taste. Add the lamb to the sauce and cook for another hour, adding extra stock if it looks dry. Keep stirring and scraping the sides. Season to taste.
4 Put pasta into a pan of salted, boiling water and cook according to packet instructions. Drain then stir through the ragù. Finish with a drizzle of olive oil and top with oregano and grated parmesan.

DOUBLE WHAMMY ARRABIATA

Serves 4

- 4 whole, fresh red chillies
- Olive oil
- 2 garlic cloves, sliced
- 3 anchovy fillets
- 1 tsp dried oregano
- 1 x 400g tin tomatoes, or 400g passata
- 400g dried pasta

Chilli pangrattato

- Large handful of torn bread
- Olive oil
- 3 garlic cloves, crushed
- 1 dried chilli, crumbled

1 Prick chillies all over with a knife and place in a large frying pan. Cover with 1cm of oil and let them sit over a really low heat. Once they've softened, pour away most of the oil (or reserve for other recipes). Add the garlic, anchovies and oregano and fry gently for a few minutes. Stir in the tomatoes, then bring to the boil. Be careful not to break the chillies.
2 Meanwhile, cook your pasta according to packet instructions and start on the chilli pangrattato. Whizz the bread with a pinch of salt until it forms fine crumbs. Add a lug of oil to a large pan on a medium heat. Add the garlic and a few pinches of dried chilli. After a minute or so add the crumbs and toss to coat everything in the garlicky oil. Keep frying for 5-7 minutes, until you've got crisp, golden breadcrumbs, then take the pan off the heat and set aside.
3 Drain the pasta, then add to the sauce and toss gently to coat. Divide between bowls, giving everyone a whole chilli, and serve sprinkled with pangrattato.

ORECCHIETTE & LAMB RAGU

CRAB LINGUINE

CRAB LINGUINE

Serves 4

- 500g linguine
- 3 tbsp olive oil
- 2 garlic cloves, sliced
- 1 tsp chilli flakes
- 16 cherry tomatoes
- 350ml tomato passata
- 600g cooked crabmeat
- Grated zest of ½ lemon

1 Bring a large pan of salted water to the boil and cook the linguine according to packet instructions.
2 Meanwhile, heat the oil in a frying pan over a medium heat. Add the garlic and chilli and sauté for 2-3 minutes, then add the tomatoes and tomato passata and cook for 5-7 minutes. Add the crab, lemon zest, season and combine well.
3 When the linguine is al dente, add to the pan, toss to combine with the sauce, then serve immediately.

FRIED RICE

Serves 2-3

- 2 eggs
- 2 spring onions, chopped
- 3 tbsp sunflower or groundnut oil
- 2 red chillies, finely sliced
- 150g mangetouts, sugarsnap peas or baby corn (or a mixture), sliced
- 500g cooked basmatic or jasmine rice (about 250g uncooked)
- 1-2 tbsp soy sauce
- Juice of ½ lime (optional)

1 Whisk the eggs with the spring onions. Put a wok on a high heat and, when very hot, add the oil and fry the red chillies with your vegetables for 1-2 minutes. Stir in the soy sauce, then add the cooked rice, stirring to combine. Pour in the whisked eggs and spring onions down the side of the wok, tilt the pan, then quickly stir to combine. Continue to fry the rice until the eggs set and bits of the rice are crisping up and turning golden. Remove from heat and squeeze over lime juice, if desired. Taste, adjust seasoning with more soy sauce if needed, and serve immediately. For more ideas, see the box on page 74.

FRIED RICE

More Italian inspiration

Some of the simplest Italian pasta dishes use combinations of beans and pulses for sauces. In Naples, lampi e tuoni (lightning and thunder) traditionally pairs a thin, broken lasagne-style pasta with chickpeas, chilli flakes and parsley. Orechiette with lentils is common in Apulia, while bean and pasta soups are found throughout Italy. Sicily has some of the most exciting but simple pasta recipes - pasta alla norma is a satisfying summer dish of rigatoni with aubergine, tomato, basil and ricotta. On this southern Italian island you'll also find all sorts of pasta cooked with cauliflower, artichokes or broccoli, often enlivened with anchovies and breadcrumbs. Classic Sicilian seafood pastas include pasta con le sarde, which is bucatini with fresh sardines, fennel, currants, pine nuts, saffron and breadcrumbs, or penne with *pesce spada* (swordfish), green olives and capers, and spaghetti with prawns, tomato and marsala.

COLD SOBA NOODLES

COLD SOBA NOODLES

Serves 2 as an entrée
- 200g soba noodles
- 6 shallots or spring onions, trimmed and julienned
- ½ cucumber, sliced
- Pickled ginger (see note)
- 1 tbsp shredded toasted nori (see note)
- Soy sauce, to serve

1 Boil the soba noodles, drain and cool in iced water. Drain well and arrange on plates with the vegetables and pickled ginger to taste. Sprinkle the nori on top. Serve with soy sauce.
Note Pickled ginger and toasted nori sheets can be bought in larger supermarkets and Japanese food shops.

PORK TONKATSU & NOODLES

Serves 4
- 2 tbsp plain flour, seasoned
- 100g fresh, fine breadcrumbs
- 1 egg, beaten
- 4 x 120g pork fillets, bashed out to 1cm thick
- Vegetable oil, for frying
- 300g udon noodles
- 1 small carrot, shredded or very thinly sliced with a speed peeler
- ½ Asian or pointed cabbage, finely shredded
- 1 red chilli (optional), finely chopped
- Soy sauce and mustard, to serve

1 Put the flour on a large flat plate, the breadcrumbs on another and the beaten egg in a shallow bowl. Take one pork fillet, dip it first in the flour, shaking off any excess, then in the egg and lastly coat in the breadcrumbs. Repeat with the other pork fillets.
2 Meanwhile, boil a saucepan of water and cook the udon noodles according to packet instructions. When done, drain and toss with carrot and cabbage and soy sauce to taste. Transfer to bowls.
3 Meanwhile, in a large frying pan over a medium heat, add a good lug of vegetable oil, heat until sizzling and then add the pork fillets. Cook for 3-4 minutes on each side, until golden-brown. You will probably have to do this in batches. Drain on kitchen paper before slicing. Top noodles with sliced pork and serve immediately with extra soy sauce and mustard.

Our wine match

Make a luxurious lobster salad even more indulgent with a glass of smooth, fragrant Canepa Classico Chardonnay. Go to page 170 for more details of our great wine offer.

FISH & SEAFOOD

TAKING INSPIRATION FROM THE OCEANS OF THE WORLD

We love fish any way – raw, as salmon tartare (page 90),
lightly cured in ceviche (page 89) and in a spicy stew (page 93).
Our fin romance encompasses the global daily catch, from
Jamie's Scottish salmon with seashore veg (page 85) to prawns
with Middle Eastern (page 78) and Indian (page 81) flavours

TROUT WITH HAM & CIDER

CRAB CAKES

TROUT WITH HAM & CIDER

Serves 2

- 2 whole fresh trout
- 1 thick slice of ham, julienned
- 1 tbsp finely chopped parsley
- Plain flour, for dusting
- 1 knob of butter
- 1 tbsp olive oil
- 1 glass of dry cider

1 Season the trout and place half the ham and parsley in the stomach cavities. Carefully roll the trout in flour. Over a medium heat, melt the butter and oil in a frying pan that fits both fish. Fry the trout for 5 minutes on each side, until cooked and golden on the outside.
2 Add the cider and cook for 2 minutes, till cider is bubbling and reducing. Scatter over remaining ham and parsley. Place on plates and drizzle with sauce left in pan.

CRAB CAKES

Makes about 10

- 750g cooked crabmeat
- 300g mashed potatoes
- 3 spring onions, chopped
- 2 tbsp finely chopped parsley
- 1 tsp each ground white pepper and cayenne
- 1 beaten egg
- Flour, for dusting
- Olive oil, for frying
- Watercress and tartare sauce, to serve

1 Combine crabmeat, potatoes, onion, parsley, pepper, cayenne and egg in a bowl with a little salt. Refrigerate for 30 minutes. Shape into 6cm cakes. Dust with flour and shallow-fry in olive oil over a medium heat for about 5 minutes each side or until golden-brown. Serve with watercress and tartare sauce.

BBQ PRAWNS, RAS EL HANOUT & LENTIL SALAD

Recipe by Greg Malouf, Momo, Melbourne, Australia
Serves 6 as a starter

- 12 raw king prawns, shell on
- 60ml olive oil

Golden ras el hanout

- 1 tbsp coriander seeds
- 1 tbsp cumin seeds
- 1 tbsp turmeric
- 1 tsp each chilli powder and ground ginger

Lentil salad

- 100g puy lentils, washed
- 100ml extra-virgin olive oil
- Juice of 2 lemons
- 2 tomatoes, deseeded and cut into 1cm dice
- 1 medium red onion, finely diced
- 40g pitted kalamata olives, sliced
- 1 tbsp chopped thyme leaves
- 2 tbsp chopped flat-leaf parsley

1 To make the ras el hanout, lightly roast then grind the coriander and cumin seeds. Sieve to remove the husks and combine in a bowl with remaining spices.
2 Cook the lentils in lots of unsalted water for 30 minutes, or until tender. Drain well, then return to the saucepan. While still warm, stir in the olive oil and lemon juice and season with salt and black pepper. Set aside for 10 minutes.
3 Peel the prawns, leaving the heads and tails intact. With a knife, split along the back and pull away any black intestines. Dust the prawns lightly with the ras el hanout and season with salt and black pepper. Brush with olive oil and cook on a preheated barbecue or griddle for 2 minutes each side, or until cooked, pink and firm.
4 Meanwhile, warm lentils gently over a low heat. Stir in chopped tomatoes, onion, olives and herbs and heat briefly. Place prawns in a mound in the centre of a serving platter. Spoon the lentil salad over and around them, drizzling over a little more olive oil, if desired.

BBQ PRAWNS, RAS EL HANOUT & LENTIL SALAD

MALABAR PRAWN CURRY

MALABAR PRAWN CURRY

Recipe by Deep Mohan Singh Arneja
Serves 2

- 4 tbsp coconut oil (or vegetable oil)
- ½ tsp black mustard seeds
- ¼ tsp fenugreek seeds
- 1 tbsp chopped fresh ginger
- 12 curry leaves, fresh or dried
- 3 small red onions, finely chopped
- 1 tsp chilli powder
- 1 tbsp ground coriander
- ¼ tsp ground turmeric
- 150g tomato, chopped
- 1 tbsp kokum powder (or 20g tamarind pulp)
- 12 raw king prawns, peeled
- 400ml coconut milk
- 2 dried red chillies
- Basmati rice, to serve

1 Heat 3 tbsp oil in a frying pan, and when it's almost smoking, add half the mustard seeds, the fenugreek seeds, ginger and half the curry leaves. Stir-fry for a few seconds, then add the onion and cook over a medium heat until a dark golden colour.
2 Add the chilli powder, coriander and turmeric, and stir for a few seconds. Add the tomato and kokum (or tamarind pulp). Simmer until slightly reduced and you can start to see the oil separating from the sauce. Add a few tablespoons of water to get the sauce back to the consistency it was before, season with salt and add the prawns. Simmer until the prawns are cooked through and the sauce is quite dry, then add the coconut milk, bring back to boil and then turn the heat down to low.
3 In another pan, heat 1 tablespoon of oil, the dried chillies, and remaining mustard seeds and curry leaves. Fry for 10 seconds or so, then tip into the curry. Serve with basmati rice.

MACKEREL & STEWED CAULIFLOWER

MACKEREL & STEWED CAULIFLOWER

Recipe by April Bloomfield
Serves 4

- 4 mackerel fillets, skin on
- Lemon juice
- 1 red chilli, chopped

Stewed cauliflower
- 3 tbsp olive oil
- 1 head cauliflower cut into large florets, plus greens if tender
- 3 garlic cloves, halved
- 4 anchovy fillets
- 1 x 400g tin chopped tomatoes

1 For the cauliflower, heat the olive oil in a large saucepan, add the cauliflower and cook until brown. Add the garlic and cauliflower greens, if using, and cook until toasty, then add the anchovies and cook for a few minutes until they have melted. Add the tomatoes and season with sea salt and freshly ground black pepper. Continue to cook until the cauliflower is tender.
2 Meanwhile, season the mackerel with salt, then dry fry skin-side down in a hot pan just long enough to crisp the skin. Remove from the heat (the fish will continue to cook in the hot pan). Using a spatula, gently turn the fish, squeeze over lemon juice and sprinkle with chilli. Serve with the stewed cauliflower.

HADDOCK, SPINACH & EGG

POTTED CRAB & SHRIMP

Serves 4

- 300g unsalted butter
- Generous grating of nutmeg
- Pinch of mace
- Pinch of cayenne pepper
- 250g cooked peeled brown shrimp
- 250g picked crabmeat (a mixture of white and brown meat)
- Zest of 1 lemon, finely grated
- 2-3 sprigs of dill or fennel tops
- Small loaf of rye bread, thinly sliced and toasted, and lemon wedges, to serve

1 Melt 100g butter in a saucepan, add the spices and good pinches of sea salt and ground white pepper. Allow to cool slightly, then add the seafood and lemon zest and mix well. Divide between ramekins or bowls and push down flat, leaving at least 1cm at the top of each. 2 Melt the rest of the butter, skimming off any white froth from the top. Once melted, allow to cool a little, then pour over the top of the pots. Pull some fronds off the dill or fennel tops and scatter over the melted butter, grate over a little more nutmeg and chill in the fridge for at least an hour. Like this, they will keep for up to a week. To serve, crack off the buttery lids and spoon the potted goodness onto little rye toasts. Even better with a glass of chablis.

HADDOCK, SPINACH & EGG

Serves 2

- 2 x 150g smoked haddock fillets
- 2 bay leaves
- 300g spinach
- 2 eggs
- Milk, for poaching
- Freshly grated nutmeg

1 Place haddock in shallow pan, add the bay leaves and enough milk to cover the fillets and bring gently to the boil. Cover, reduce heat and simmer very gently for about 5 minutes, until the fish is cooked and flakes easily. Remove the fish from the milk, cover and keep warm. 2 Steam or pan-fry the spinach until just cooked. Drain off any excess liquid and season well with salt and pepper and a little grated nutmeg, then keep warm. 3 Meanwhile, poach the eggs in water for 3-4 minutes, making sure not to overcook them - you want the yolks to remain soft. Transfer haddock and spinach to plates and top with an egg.

FISH BAKED IN SALT

BAKED SALMON SALAD

Serves 8 as an entrée

- 800g salmon fillet, scaled, pin-boned
- 1–2 lemons
- Olive oil
- 2 slices good-quality stale bread, torn
- Small handful of fresh basil leaves
- 5 tbsp good-quality mayonnaise
- 400g broad beans, podded
- 1 bunch of sea kale or 260g spinach
- 200g samphire or baby asparagus
- 2 handfuls of mixed baby salad leaves, such as watercress, rocket, dandelion and any edible shoots
- Extra-virgin olive oil
- Lemon wedges and warm bread, to serve

1 Preheat the oven to 180C/gas 4. Season salmon with salt, pepper and grated lemon zest. Drizzle with olive oil and the juice of half a lemon, then rub into the fish. Put 2 pieces of foil in an earthenware dish and lay salmon in middle. Seal edges to make a parcel, bake for 20 minutes, then remove from oven and stand for 20 minutes.
2 Add bread to a food processor with a little olive oil, salt and pepper. Pulse to chunky breadcrumbs, place in a tray and bake for 10 minutes, till lightly golden.
3 Bash up the basil and stir through the mayo with a squeeze of lemon juice.
4 Add broad beans and sea kale to a pan of salted boiling water and cook for 2 minutes, then add samphire and cook for a minute. (If using asparagus and spinach, cook asparagus with beans, then add spinach for last 30 seconds.) Drain, then let cool on a tray. Dress with olive oil, lemon juice, salt and pepper.
5 Once everything is ready, open the foil parcel and put flakes of salmon on each plate. Season to taste, add a tiny squeeze of lemon, then dollop a good spoonful of basil mayo in the middle. Sprinkle over some breadcrumbs. Have a taste of the cooled veg to check the seasoning, then dollop on some mayo.
6 Dress salad leaves with extra-virgin olive oil, salt, pepper and a squeeze of lemon, then sit a big pinch of it on top of the seashore veg. Serve immediately with lemon wedges and warm bread.

BAKED SALMON SALAD

FISH BAKED IN SALT

Serves 2

- 500g lemon salt (see page 160)
- 500g chilli salt (see page 160)
- 2 egg whites
- 1 x 550g sea bass, cleaned
- 1 x 550g black bream, cleaned
- 2–3 bay leaves
- 2–3 sprigs of fresh thyme
- Lemon wedges and extra-virgin olive oil, to serve

1 Preheat the oven to 200C/gas 6. Combine the lemon salt with one egg white in a bowl, and the chilli salt and remaining egg white in another bowl.
2 Spread a layer of half of each salt mixture over each half of the base of a large oval ovenproof dish. Place the fish on top then cover with remaining salt mixtures. Stick the bay and thyme into the salt and bake for 40 minutes.
3 Remove the fish from the oven and cool for a few minutes, then, using a knife, break salt crust and discard. Scrape off the fish skin and remove the flesh from the bones. Serve with lemon wedges and a drizzle of olive oil.

SUMMER FISH PIE

mint leaves, add to the pan, then squash the potatoes to a chunky mash and spread over the pie. Place pie in the oven for 35 minutes, until golden-brown and bubbling. Let the pie cool slightly before serving scattered with fennel fronds, and with ketchup and vegetables.

SPICY SOFT-SHELL CRAB

Recipe from Jamie's Italian
Serves 8 as a starter

- 1 litre vegetable oil, for deep-frying
- 400g Italian '00' flour
- 30g hot smoked paprika
- 30g fennel seeds, toasted, ground
- 500g plain yoghurt
- Juice of 1 lemon
- 8 soft-shell crabs (see note), cleaned
- Sweet paprika and parsley, to serve

Spicy Amalfi mayo

- ½ beef tomato, deseeded and diced
- ¼ carrot, finely diced
- ½ stalk of celery, finely diced
- 3 green olives, flesh finely diced
- 2 cornichons, finely diced
- ¼ each of red onion, fennel, courgette, yellow pepper and red pepper, all finely diced
- 3 anchovy fillets, finely diced
- 1 red chilli, deseeded and chopped
- Small handful of parsley, finely chopped
- 15ml olive oil
- Juice of 1 lemon
- 250ml mayonnaise
- 50ml tomato ketchup

1 To make spicy mayo, combine all ingredients. Season to taste.
2 In a deep saucepan, heat oil to 180C, or when a cube of potato rises to the top and turns golden brown. (Never leave hot fat unattended and be very careful when deep-frying.) Combine flour, hot paprika and fennel seeds on a plate, and the yoghurt, lemon juice and some salt on another. Coat crabs in yoghurt, then dust in flour. Repeat. Carefully fry crabs for 8 minutes, turning. Remove, drain on kitchen paper, and sprinkle with salt and sweet paprika. Serve with parsley, spicy mayo and lemon wedges.
Note Soft-shells, crabs that have moulted, are available frozen from good fishmongers or South-East Asian shops.

SUMMER FISH PIE

Serves 8-10

- Bunch of fresh mint
- 2kg new potatoes, scrubbed clean
- 2 bulbs of fennel, finely sliced, tops reserved
- Olive oil
- Knob of butter, plus extra
- 3 leeks, trimmed and sliced
- ½ red chilli, deseeded and sliced
- ½ glass white wine
- 2 tsp English mustard
- 2 fresh bay leaves
- 600g each salmon fillet and smoked haddock, skinned and pinboned
- 400g frozen prawns
- 200ml single cream
- Juice of 1 lemon
- 150g grated parmesan cheese
- Tomato ketchup and asparagus, peas or beans to serve

1 Pick the mint leaves from the stalks and put them to one side. Add the stalks to a large pan of salted boiling water with the potatoes and cook for 10 minutes or until they're tender.
2 Pop the fennel tops on a plate and put in the fridge with the mint leaves until later. Preheat the oven to 200C/gas 6. Add a lug of olive oil and knob of butter to an appropriately sized casserole pan, then add your leeks, fennel bulbs and chilli, then season. Cook for 10 minutes, till the vegetables have softened, then add the wine, mustard and bay leaves.
3 Cook the wine away, then take the pan off the heat. Slice the fish into 2.5cm pieces and sprinkle into the pan with the prawns. Stir in the cream, lemon juice and parmesan, then carefully season.
4 Drain the potatoes, discarding mint, and return to the pan with some butter, olive oil and seasoning. Finely chop the

SEAS BASS & GRAPEFRUIT CEVICHE

SWORDFISH WITH CAPERS

SEA BASS & GRAPEFRUIT CEVICHE

Serves 4

- 500g very fresh sea bass, scaled, filleted and pinboned
- Juice of 2 lemons
- 2 fresh red chillies, halved, deseeded and chopped into 1cm rounds
- 1 garlic clove, grated or finely chopped
- 2 pink grapefruits
- 2 heads of fennel, trimmed and cut into thin wedges, tops reserved
- Small bunch of mint, leaves picked
- Extra-virgin olive oil, for drizzling

1 Slice the fish into 1cm strips, put them in a bowl and refrigerate. In a separate bowl, mix the lemon juice, chilli, garlic and a teaspoon of salt then chill this too.
2 Cut the top and bottom off the grapefruit, then carefully peel away the skin and separate the fruit into segments. Put the grapefruit segments in a bowl, squeezing the juice from a few of them into the bowl.
3 When your guests are ready to eat, take the fish out of the fridge and combine it with the fennel wedges, grapefruit segments and most of the mint leaves. Give the marinade in the bowl or jam jar a mix, then pour the juices over the fish mixture. Delicately toss together and allow to marinate for just 2½ minutes.
4 Serve very simply, on a big platter, with the remaining mint leaves and fennel tops sprinkled over, adding a little drizzle of olive oil and a few grinds of black pepper.

SWORDFISH WITH CAPERS

Serves 2

- 2 swordfish steaks
- Olive oil
- 2 cloves garlic, finely sliced
- 20 cherry tomatoes
- 1 lemon, peeled and segmented
- 50g capers
- Finely chopped flat-leaf parsley

1 Season swordfish, drizzle with olive oil then pan-fry or grill over a high heat until cooked, about 5 minutes on each side. Transfer to plates. Heat oil in a frying pan over a high heat, add garlic and tomatoes and sauté for 5 minutes. Add lemon and capers and cook for 2 minutes. Add parsley, season and stir, then pour over fish and serve.

SALMON TARTARE

SALMON TARTARE

Serves 4

- 500g salmon fillet, very finely diced
- ¼ tsp mustard powder
- Juice of ½ lemon
- 1 tbsp finely chopped chives
- 1 tbsp capers, plus extra to serve
- 2 finely chopped shallots
- 1 tbsp extra-virgin olive oil
- Cornichons and crispbread, to serve

1 In a bowl, combine the diced salmon, mustard powder, lemon juice, chives, capers, shallots and olive oil, then season to taste with sea salt and freshly ground black pepper. Press into 4 ramekins or moulds, then turn out onto plates. Serve with the cornichons, extra capers and Swedish crispbread.

FISH & TOMATOES EN PAPILLOTE

Recipe by Rodney Dunn, The Agrarian Kitchen, Tasmania, Australia
Serves 4

- 4 x 200g fillets of firm white-fleshed fish, such as bream or cod
- 400g heirloom tomatoes, cut into 2cm pieces
- 2 garlic cloves, thinly sliced
- 4 bay leaves
- 3 spring onions, thinly sliced
- 2 tbsp extra-virgin olive oil
- 8 basil leaves, torn or sliced

1 Preheat the oven to 180C/gas 4. Place a piece of fish in the centre of a large piece of non-stick baking paper. Scatter with some of the tomatoes and some each of the garlic, bay leaves and spring onion. Season to taste with sea salt and freshly ground black pepper. Drizzle with extra-virgin olive oil and scatter with some torn basil. Fold up the sides and then either tuck in or tie up with string to seal.
2 Repeat with the remaining ingredients until you have 4 parcels. Place the parcels on a baking tray and roast in the oven for 15–18 minutes or until fish is just cooked through. Place parcels on plates to be opened at the table and serve immediately.

FISH & TOMATOES EN PAPILLOTE

AWESOME ASIAN FISH STEW

Serves 4

- 300–350g jasmine or basmati rice
- Peeled zest and juice of 2 limes
- 1–2 tbsp sesame oil
- 1 x 400ml tin coconut milk
- 250ml organic chicken stock
- 5–6 dried birds-eye chillies
- 4 langoustines
- 400g monkfish, cut into 1cm slices
- 8 queen scallops, or 4 large scallops, halved
- Soy sauce

Spice paste

- 2 thumb-sized pieces of ginger, peeled
- 8 lime leaves
- 2 fresh mild red chillies
- 4 garlic cloves
- 2 lemongrass stalks
- Small bunch of fresh coriander
- 1 level tsp sweet chilli powder
- 2 tbsp groundnut oil

1 Add all your paste ingredients to a mortar or blender and pound or blitz until you've got a thick, aromatic paste. **2** Get a large pan of water on to boil. Rinse the rice in a sieve under running water for about a minute, or until the water runs clear (this will stop the grains sticking together). Add the lime zest to the boiling water along with the rice and wait for the grains to start dancing around. From that point, boil for 5 minutes, then drain the rice in a sieve. Pour 2.5cm of water into the pan, put it back on the heat and bring up to the boil again, then turn down to a simmer. Cover the rice in the sieve with tin foil and place on top of the pan for 8–10 minutes – check at 8 minutes. The rice should now be ready to serve. **3** Meanwhile, place another large saucepan over a medium heat, add in the sesame oil, then the spice paste, and fry for a minute or two to get the flavours going. Add the coconut milk, chicken stock and lime juice. Give everything a good stir, add the dried chillies, bring to the boil and turn down to a simmer. Let it cook for 5 minutes, then add the langoustines and cook them for 3 minutes. Now add the fish and scallops and cook for 3 more minutes. Add a few dashes of soy sauce to season to your taste. The fish won't need long at all, so once it's cooked through and the langoustines have turned bright red and their tails have curled up, take the stew off the heat. **4** Put a spoonful of rice into each of the serving bowls, then ladle the fish stew over the top, making sure everyone gets a langoustine and some nice pieces of fish and scallops. Just watch out for those dried chillies!

HARISSA PRAWNS

HARISSA PRAWNS

Serves 2

- 2 tbsp of rose harissa (see note)
- 12 large king prawns, peeled
- Hummus and flatbread, to serve

1 In a bowl, combine the rose harissa with the king prawns. Thread 3 prawns onto each of 4 wooden skewers. Char-grill or barbecue the prawns for 3–4 minutes on each side, or until cooked through. Serve with hummus and warm flatbread.

Note Rose petals add a delicate fragrance to harissa. Rose harissa is available from specialist delicatessens and Middle Eastern shops.

RED MULLET WITH TOMATOES & OLIVES

RED MULLET WITH TOMATOES & OLIVES

Serves 4

- 4 red mullet, gutted, scaled and skin slashed
- Olive oil
- 1 tbsp sweet paprika
- 2 lemons
- 500g new potatoes (optional)
- 350g cherry tomatoes, some halved
- Good handful of pitted black olives
- 3 garlic cloves, finely sliced

1 Preheat oven to 220C/gas 7. Rub the fish with oil and season inside and out with the paprika, sea salt and black pepper. Grate over the lemon zest.
2 If using new potatoes, bring a large pan of salted water to the boil. Add the potatoes and boil for 10-15 minutes until just tender. Drain.
3 Slice the zested lemons and add to a baking tray with the tomatoes, olives, sliced garlic and new potatoes (if using). Place the seasoned fish on top, drizzle with olive oil then bake for 15 minutes, or until the fish is cooked through. Serve with a nice green salad and a glass of crisp white wine.

THAI MUSSELS

Serves 2

- 1kg mussels, washed and debearded
- Groundnut oil
- 4 spring onions, finely sliced
- 2 garlic cloves, finely sliced
- Small bunch of coriander, stalks finely chopped, leaves picked
- 1 lemongrass stick, cut into 4
- 1 red chilli, finely sliced
- 400ml coconut milk
- 1 tbsp fish sauce
- 1 lime

1 Discard mussels that aren't tightly closed. In a saucepan, heat a little groundnut oil and soften spring onions, garlic, coriander stalks, lemongrass and most of the chilli for around 5 minutes. Add coconut milk and fish sauce and bring to the boil. Add mussels and cover pan. Steam for 5 minutes, till mussels are open and cooked. Discard any unopened mussels. Finish with a squeeze of lime, and sprinkle with coriander leaves and remaining chilli.

THAI MUSSELS

Our wine match
This flinty Domaine Cristia Grenache is fantastic with roast chicken with all the trimmings. Go to page 170 for more details about our great wine club offer.

MEAT & POULTRY

IF IT CLUCKED, QUACKED, OINKED OR MOOED, WE'RE COOKING IT

Whether you want a light lunch, like steak wraps (page 113), or game stews of rabbit (page 102) and pheasant (page 126), there's plenty to sink your teeth into. Our recipes sure to please the family include burgers (page 98), roast lamb (page 105) and the best fried chicken from the state of Kentucky (page 118)

ROAST PORK LOIN

BUTTER BEAN & CHORIZO STEW

ROAST PORK LOIN

Serves 10

- 2.5kg pork loin, skin off, bones trimmed and tied with kitchen string
- 2 garlic heads, tops sliced off
- 2–3 fresh bay leaves
- 6 fresh thyme sprigs
- 2 tbsp extra-virgin olive oil

1 Preheat the oven to 200C/gas 6. Place pork and garlic in a roasting tin. Tuck bay leaves and thyme under string on pork. Season with salt and black pepper. Drizzle with olive oil and roast for 2 hours. Remove from oven and rest for 10 minutes before carving.

BUTTER BEAN & CHORIZO STEW

Serves 4

- 200g chorizo, sliced
- 2 red onions, sliced
- 3 garlic cloves, sliced
- Olive oil
- 1 tsp smoked paprika
- 1 x 400g tin tomatoes
- 1 x 400g tin butter beans

1 In a medium saucepan over a medium heat, cook the chorizo, onion and garlic in a little olive oil for 5 minutes. Add in the paprika, tomatoes and beans, then reduce the heat, cover and cook for 20 minutes. Remove the lid in the last few minutes to thicken stew, if desired. Serve with slices of crusty bread and a nice glass of red wine.

CHILLI BURGERS

Serves 4

- Olive oil
- 1 ciabatta, split lengthways
- Pinch of smoked paprika
- 5 garlic cloves, 4 smashed, 1 minced
- 500g good-quality beef mince
- 2 dried chipotle chillies, rehydrated in water then roughly chopped
- 4 spring onions, finely sliced
- 1 egg, beaten
- Handful of fresh breadcrumbs
- Salad and condiments (lettuce, tomatoes, red onions, cornichons, American-style mustard and ketchup), to serve

1 Preheat your oven to 180C/gas 4. Drizzle olive oil over the cut sides of the ciabatta, then rub with paprika and smashed garlic. Place bread on a tray and bake for 5 minutes, or until golden.
2 In a bowl, combine beef, chillies, onion, minced garlic, egg and breadcrumbs. Mix well, fry a teaspoon and taste to check seasoning. Shape into 4 patties.
3 Get a frying or griddle pan to a medium-high heat, then drizzle in some olive oil and cook burgers for 5 minutes on each side for medium-rare, or until done to your liking. Slice ciabatta loaf into 4, then make your burgers with your choice of accompaniments.

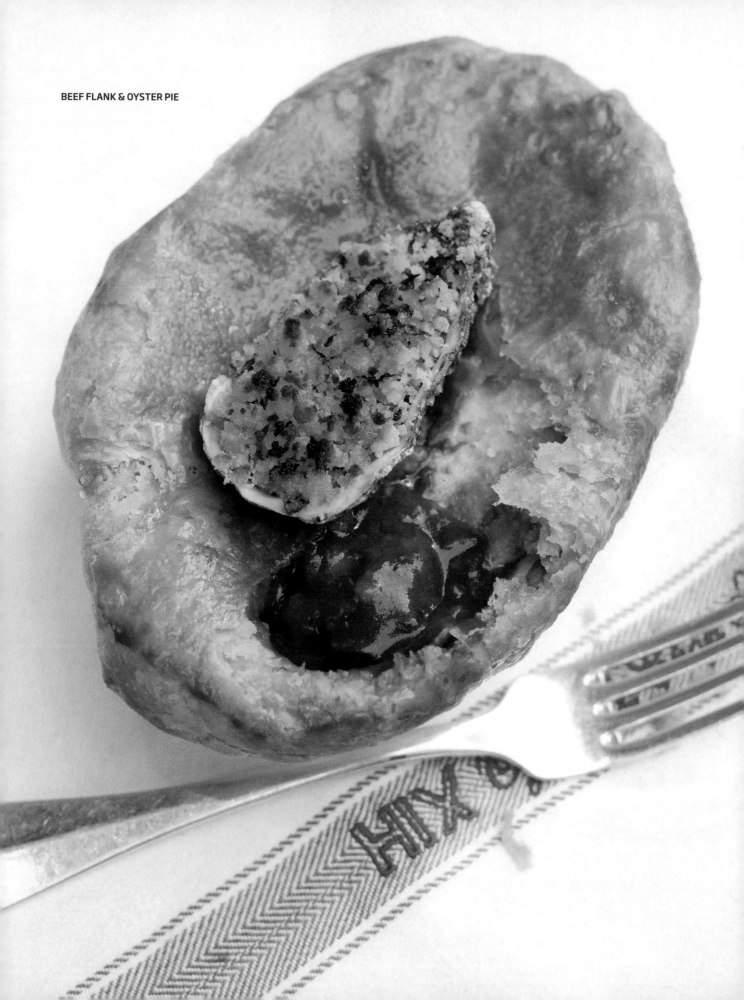

BEEF FLANK & OYSTER PIE

PHEASANT WITH BRUSCHETTA

Recipe by Gennaro Contaldo
Serves 4

- 2 pheasants – ask your butcher to chop them into medium-sized pieces (and include the liver, kidney and ribs)
- Plain flour, for dusting
- 150ml extra-virgin olive oil
- 1 garlic bulb, cloves separated but skins left on
- 2 whole red chillies, sliced in half lengthways and deseeded
- Bunch of rosemary, broken in half
- 150ml white wine

Bruschetta
- Slices of ciabatta
- Cut garlic cloves

1 Season pheasant and dust with flour. Heat oil in a heavy-based pan. Add pheasant and seal until golden-brown and crisp. Reduce heat, add garlic, chillies and rosemary, cover and cook for 30 minutes, turning occasionally. Raise heat to high, remove lid, add the wine and simmer until evaporated.
2 For the bruschetta, toast ciabatta, rub with cut garlic and drizzle with some of the oil that has risen to the top of the pheasant sauce. Serve pheasant with bruschetta and some of the sauce.

PHEASANT WITH BRUSCHETTA

BEEF FLANK & OYSTER PIE

Recipe by Mark Hix,
Hix Oyster & Chop House, London
Makes 4 individual pies

- Vegetable oil, for frying
- 2 tbsp plain flour
- 900g trimmed beef flank (or shin or ox cheek), cut into rough 3cm cubes
- 1 medium onion, finely chopped
- 1 garlic clove, roughly chopped
- 1 tsp tomato purée
- 200ml porter or Guinness
- 1 litre beef stock
- 1 tsp chopped thyme leaves
- 1 small bay leaf
- 1 tsp cornflour (optional)
- 12 oysters, 8 shucked, 4 on the shell

Cold-water crust pastry
- 225g self-raising flour, plus extra
- 85g shredded beef suet
- 60g butter, chilled and grated
- 1 medium egg, beaten

Parsley crust for oysters
- Good knob of butter
- 4 tbsp fresh white breadcrumbs
- 1 tbsp chopped parsley

1 Heat oil in a heavy frying pan, lightly flour meat and season. Fry in batches over a high heat till browned. Set aside.
2 Fry onions and garlic for a few minutes, stir in tomato purée and remaining flour over a low heat for a minute or so. Slowly stir in porter and stock. Add herbs and beef, bring to the boil, cover and simmer for 2 hours, till meat is tender. If sauce is thin, mix 1 teaspoon of cornflour into a paste with water, stir into sauce and simmer for a few minutes. Let mixture cool and pour into four 280ml capacity pie dishes to about 1cm from the top.

3 To make pastry, mix flour and a teaspoon of salt with suet and butter. Mix in 150–175ml cold water to form a smooth dough and knead for a minute. Roll out on a floured table to about 7mm thick. Cut out 4 discs about 2cm larger all the way round than the dishes. Make a 2cm hole in the middle of each. Brush edges with beaten egg and lay pastry over dishes, pressing egg-washed side against the dish. Brush tops with egg.
4 Rest in a cool place for 15 minutes and preheat oven to 200C/gas 6. Bake pies for 30 minutes. Add two shucked oysters to each pie through holes in crusts and bake for a further 10 minutes.
5 To make parsley crust, melt butter in a pan, mix in breadcrumbs and parsley. Season. Scatter the parsley mixture over the oysters on the half-shell. Grill until golden. Serve pies with an oyster over each hole.

LAPIN MADAME COTS

- 4 stalks of rosemary, plus extra, to serve
- 2 garlic cloves, finely chopped
- 1 red dutch or other long chilli, halved
- 6 red cherry tomatoes, quartered
- 6 yellow cherry tomatoes, quartered
- 200g tinned tomatoes
- 1 tbsp capers
- Large handful of kalamata olives

1 Wrap two bricks in foil. Get a grill pan nice and hot (depending on the size of your pan, you might have to use two pans or cook the chicken in batches). Place the chicken on a board. Oil and season both sides. Divide the chicken into 2 pieces. With a meat hammer or rolling pin, pummel the rosemary into the flesh to release its oils. Place the chicken halves skin-side down onto the char-grill and place the bricks on top of the chicken to weigh it down. (You could also use a cast-iron saucepan or a heavy lid that's smaller than the pan to squash the chicken.) Grill for 10 minutes each side. (If you aren't using bricks, char-grill the chicken halves for 4 minutes each side, or until golden, and then put in an oven preheated to 200C/gas 6 for 15 minutes.) When the chicken is crisp-skinned, golden-brown and cooked through, place it on a metal tray in a warm place and allow to rest.
2 Meanwhile, heat ½ tablespoon of olive oil in a hot frying pan, then add the garlic and chilli and cook until golden. Add the cherry tomatoes and cook for 2 minutes, then add the tinned tomatoes, capers and olives. Cook for another 2 minutes, then season to taste with sea salt and freshly ground black pepper. Remove the chilli halves.
3 To serve, put the tomato sauce on a platter. Cut up the chicken halves and place them on top of the tomatoes, then pour over the resting juices, scatter over some rosemary sprigs or chopped leaves, and drizzle with a little extra-virgin olive oil.

LAPIN MADAME COTS

Recipe from Danny Moynihan
Serves 4

- Small handful of peppercorns
- 5 garlic cloves
- 5 cloves
- 3 tbsp red wine vinegar
- 8 tbsp olive oil
- 1 rabbit, including liver, kidneys and heart, cut into 8 pieces – ask your butcher to cut the hind legs in 2, but leave kidneys attached to the saddle
- 800g potatoes, quartered
- 3 tbsp chopped flat-leaf parsley

1 In a mortar, crush the peppercorns, garlic and cloves. Add the vinegar and 5 tabespoons of olive oil. Mix well.
2 Heat remaining oil in a casserole on a medium heat and fry rabbit pieces for 3-5 minutes, until browned. Season with salt. Turn heat up to high, pour in sauce mixture, let vinegar evaporate then add 8 tablespoons of water. Cook, stirring, for 30 seconds, then turn heat right down. Simmer gently for 40 minutes.
3 Meanwhile, add potatoes to a pan of salted water, bring to the boil and cook for 15 minutes, until tender. Drain and add to the casserole along with parsley. Cook for a further 10 minutes and serve.

CHICKEN COOKED UNDER A BRICK

Recipe from Jamie's Italian
Serves 4

- 1 chicken, boned (ask your butcher to do this for you)
- Extra-virgin olive oil

CHILLI-OREGANO LAMB SHOULDER

CHICKEN KOKKINISTO

Serves 6

- 50ml extra-virgin olive oil
- 1kg baby onions, peeled
- 1 onion, sliced
- 4 garlic cloves, sliced
- 1 free-range chicken, cut into 6 pieces
- Plain flour, for dusting
- 1 x 400g tin chopped tomatoes
- 1 tbsp tomato purée
- 3 fresh bay leaves
- 1 cinnamon stick
- 5 whole cloves
- ½ tbsp crushed allspice berries
- ½ tbsp dried oregano
- 2 glasses of dry red wine
- 1 tbsp red wine vinegar

1 Heat the olive oil in a cast-iron casserole dish over a medium heat and sauté onions and garlic for 5 minutes. Transfer to a bowl. Dust the chicken pieces in flour and sauté for 5-7 minutes until browned. Return the onions to the casserole dish and season to taste with salt and pepper. Add the tomatoes, tomato purée, herbs and spices, stir well and cook for 10 minutes. Season, add wine and vinegar, then simmer for 1 hour until the chicken is tender and the sauce has thickened.

CHILLI-OREGANO LAMB SHOULDER

Serves 6

- 1 shoulder of lamb (approx 2kg)

Marinade

- 2 dried chillies
- 1 tbsp fennel seeds
- Large bunch of oregano, leaves only
- Strips of zest from 1 lemon
- 1 bulb of garlic, cloves unpeeled and smashed
- 5 tbsp olive oil

1 To make the marinade, use a pestle and mortar to grind the chillies and fennel seeds, with salt and pepper, to a fine powder. Add the oregano and pound to form a paste. Add the lemon zest and garlic cloves to your mortar and bash a bit more with the pestle. Gently mix in the olive oil.
2 Stab the lamb to create holes for the marinade, then pour it over, making sure the lamb is well coated. Cover and store in the fridge for up to a day, until half an hour before cooking.
3 Preheat the oven to 180C/gas 4. Place the lamb in a roasting tray, cover with foil and pop in the oven.
4 After 4 hours, remove the foil. Turn the oven to its highest setting, baste the lamb with the juices and cook for a further 20-25 minutes, until it's nice and crisp. Rest for 10 minutes before shredding (with a couple of forks).

ROAST PORK & AGRODOLCE PEPPERS

CHICKEN, LEEK & OLIVE STEW

Serves 6

- 1 chicken
- 2 onions, sliced
- 3 leeks, sliced
- 1 celery heart, sliced
- 3 garlic cloves, finely sliced
- 2 potatoes, peeled and chopped
- 15-20 large green olives
- Juice of 1 lemon
- 1 tbsp fresh thyme leaves
- 2 fresh bay leaves
- 4 tbsp olive oil
- 150ml dry white wine

1 Heat oil in a large cast-iron casserole dish. Add onions, leeks, celery, garlic, thyme and bay leaves and cook over medium heat for about 5 minutes or until softened. Transfer to a bowl. Add chicken pieces and cook, in batches if necessary, for 5-7 minutes, until golden brown. Add vegetables back to casserole dish with potatoes and olives then season with salt and black pepper. Add lemon juice and wine, and water if necessary, to just cover the mixture. Boil, then simmer over a low heat for 1 hour, until chicken is cooked and sauce has thickened. Serve with crusty bread.

ROAST PORK & AGRODOLCE PEPPERS

Serves 6

- 1 x 2kg pork belly, on the bone
- 2 tbsp fennel seeds
- Pesto (see page 164), to serve

Agrodolce peppers

- 3 anchovy fillets
- 375ml extra-virgin olive oil
- 3 garlic cloves, sliced
- 1½ red onions, sliced
- 2 bay leaves
- 750ml white wine
- 3 red peppers, sliced
- 3 yellow peppers, sliced
- 75g caster sugar
- 45ml red wine vinegar
- 75g fine capers

Colcannon

- 300g potatoes, washed
- 200g chopped greens, such as cabbage, spinach or swiss chard
- Extra-virgin olive oil

1 Preheat your oven to maximum heat. Using a sharp knife, score the skin of the pork. In a pestle and mortar, bash the fennel seeds with 1 tablespoon of sea salt and ½ teaspoon ground black pepper to a fine powder. Rub into the pork skin. Place the belly in the oven for 10 minutes, then turn down to 170C/ gas 3. Roast for 3-4 hours, till meat is meltingly soft with gorgeous crackling. **2** Meanwhile, make the peppers. Melt the anchovies in 50ml olive oil in a large frying pan over a low-medium heat, then add the garlic, onions and bay. Cook for 6 minutes, or until the onions are soft. Stir in the wine and reduce until evaporated. Add the peppers and cook slowly till softened, then push to the back of the pan. In a cup or bowl, mix the sugar and vinegar, then add to the frying pan. It should boil up a bit. Stir the peppers around the pan, add remaining oil, turn to low and cook for 30 minutes. Stir as necessary. When the peppers are soft, stir in the capers, season to taste, remove from heat and cool till needed. **3** For the colcannon, boil the potatoes in salted water until tender, then drain and return to the pan. Blanch the greens by plunging into boiling water for 2 minutes, then draining and rinsing with cold water. Over a very low heat, smash up the potatoes with the greens, stir in a drizzle of extra-virgin olive oil, and season with salt and black pepper. Cover and keep warm till ready to serve. **4** To serve, top the colcannon and peppers with a slice of pork and drizzle over a good spoonful of pesto.

JERK HAM

JERK HAM

- 3kg leg of ham
- 1 tbsp whole black peppercorns
- 1 onion, cut into wedges
- 1 bouquet garni (leek, celery, bay leaves and thyme, tied together)

Jerk seasoning
- 5 garlic cloves, finely chopped
- 5 scotch bonnet peppers, deseeded, then chopped
- 4 red shallots, diced
- Bunch of chives, chopped
- 1 tbsp caster sugar
- 12 sprigs of fresh thyme
- 3 fresh bay leaves
- 2 tbsp each ground allspice, ground nutmeg, ground cloves, sea salt
- 125ml golden rum
- 125ml malt vinegar

Glaze
- 3 tbsp marmalade
- 250ml orange juice
- 125ml golden rum

1 Preheat the oven to 160C/gas 2. Place the ham in a roasting pan and add the peppercorns, onion and bouquet garni. Add water until it comes halfway up the side of the pan. Cover the ham with foil (making a tent to allow the steam to circulate). Bake for 1½ hours or until pink and cooked through, then remove from the oven and cool for 30 minutes, remaining covered. While it's still warm, you will need to carefully remove the skin, keeping the fat attached to the ham. With a sharp knife, score the ham by making diagonal cuts across the leg. **2** To make the jerk seasoning, blend all the ingredients in a food processor until you have a smooth mixture. Rub the jerk seasoning all over the ham and scored fat. Cover in plastic wrap and refrigerate overnight or for 24 hours. **3** Preheat the oven to 180C/gas 4. Combine glaze ingredients in a bowl and set aside. Remove ham from the fridge, scrape off excess seasoning and bake for an hour. Remove from oven, brush with the glaze, then continue cooking the ham for another 30-40 minutes, basting with glaze every 10 minutes until crisp, golden and sticky.

BEEF STIFADO

BEEF STIFADO
Serves 4
- 1.5kg stewing beef, such as chuck or top rump, trimmed and cut into 7cm pieces
- 4 tbsp extra-virgin olive oil
- 24 baby onions, peeled and left whole
- 4 ripe tomatoes, peeled and roughly chopped, or 1 x 400g tin chopped tomatoes
- 1 tbsp tomato purée
- Pasta and cheese such as kefalotiri, pecorino or parmesan, to serve

Marinade
- 3 garlic cloves, sliced
- 2-3 fresh bay leaves
- 1½ tsp allspice berries
- 6 whole cloves
- 1-2 cinnamon sticks
- 1 tsp dried oregano
- 125ml dry red wine
- 4 tbsp red wine vinegar

1 Place beef in a large non-reactive bowl. Add marinade ingredients, cover and refrigerate for at least 6 hours, preferably overnight. **2** Heat oil over medium heat in a large saucepan and sauté the onions for 5 minutes or until softened. Remove with a slotted spoon and set aside. Sauté the beef, reserving the marinade, for about 8-10 minutes or until browned on all sides. Return onions to the saucepan, add the marinade mixture, tomatoes and tomato purée and enough water to just cover the stew. Season generously with sea salt and freshly ground black pepper. Bring to the boil then simmer for 1½-2 hours or until the beef is tender and the sauce has thickened. Serve with pasta and grated cheese.

RABBIT TERRINE

RABBIT TERRINE

Recipe by Stéphane Reynaud
Serves 8-10

- 1 x 500g rabbit
- 150ml port
- 80g golden sultanas
- 80g dried ceps (or other dried mushrooms)
- 300g pork loin
- 1 rabbit liver
- 300g piece bacon
- 200ml single cream
- 4 shallots, peeled and finely diced
- 2 sprigs fresh rosemary, leaves picked and chopped

1 Debone rabbit and cut meat into 1cm pieces. Warm the port in a saucepan. Place the sultanas in a bowl and pour the warm port over them. Place the ceps in a separate bowl and cover them with warm water to rehydrate them.
2 Roughly chop the pork and process with the rabbit liver and bacon in a food processor until you have a coarse mince. Place in a large bowl. Add cream and season with sea salt and freshly ground black pepper. Add rabbit, port and sultanas, well-drained ceps, shallots and rosemary. Combine mixture well.
3 Preheat oven to 180C/gas 4. Place the rabbit and pork mixture in a cast-iron terrine, cover and put the terrine in a roasting tin. Pour hot water halfway up the sides of the terrine and cook in the oven for 45 minutes. Take the lid off and cook for a further 45–50 minutes, until cooked. Remove from the oven and chill for 24 hours before serving.

PORK IN CIDER & CINNAMON

Serves 6-8

- 2kg piece of pork shoulder, crackling on, bone in
- 2 garlic bulbs, broken into cloves
- 4 cinnamon sticks
- 12 bay leaves
- 200ml cider vinegar
- 570ml dry cider, plus a little extra
- Roast potatoes, to serve

1 Preheat the oven to 200C/gas 6. Rub the pork with salt and black pepper, place in a deep ovenproof pot and roast for 40 minutes, or until the meat has taken on a bit of colour.
2 Remove the pot from the oven. Lift out the pork and place it on a tray. Spoon out any excess fat from the pot (save it for basting) and add the garlic, cinnamon and bay leaves. Return pork to the pot and pour in the vinegar and cider down the sides. Cover with a lid or foil and return to the oven.
3 Turn the oven down to 180C/gas 4 and braise the pork for 3 hours, basting occasionally with reserved fat. Add more cider if the liquid starts to get low.
4 When the pork is soft and the crackling is crisp, transfer to a serving plate. (The bones should pull away easily. If not, cook for about another 30 minutes, checking.) Break up the crackling and pull the meat apart with a fork. Ladle the liquor from the pot over the pork with the cinnamon and bay leaves, and serve with roast potatoes.

PORK IN CIDER & CINNAMON

ROAST DUCK & PLUM SAUCE

ROAST DUCK & PLUM SAUCE

Serves 6-8
- 1 x 2kg duck
- 3 tbsp dark brown sugar
- ½ tsp ground cinnamon

Plum sauce
- 400g small dark red plums, stoned
- Juice and zest of 1 orange
- 5 tbsp brown sugar
- 1 cinnamon stick

1 Preheat oven to 190C/gas 5. Put the duck on a roasting tray and score the skin, rub in the sugar and cinnamon, season and cook for 20 minutes, then turn the oven right down as low as it will go and continue to cook for another 1½ hours, basting occasionally with the fat in the tray. When the duck is well done and tender, remove from oven.
2 Meanwhile, make your plum sauce. In a pan, mix together the sauce ingredients then cook over a low heat for 15 minutes. Serve with the duck.

STEAK TAHINI WRAP

Serves 2
- 1 x 400g tin chickpeas, drained
- 1 tomato, diced
- ½ small cucumber, diced
- 1 x 250g sirloin steak
- Handful of mint leaves, chopped
- Handful of parsley leaves, chopped
- 2 tbsp olive oil
- Juice of ½ lemon
- 2 Arab-style flat breads
- Pomegranate seeds (optional), to serve

Tahini sauce
- 125ml tahini
- 3 garlic cloves, crushed
- 2 tbsp olive oil
- 125ml lemon juice
- Handful of parsley leaves, chopped

1 To make tahini sauce, mix the tahini, garlic and olive oil together, then add the lemon juice. The mixture will become extremely thick once the lemon juice is added, so dilute with a small amount of boiling water until you have a thick pouring sauce. Add the parsley and season to taste. This sauce will last up to 2 weeks in the fridge.
2 Mix chickpeas, tomato and cucumber in a bowl. Add the herbs, olive oil, lemon juice and season with salt and pepper.
3 Season the steak with salt and pepper. Heat a lightly oiled grill pan and cook the steak for 3-4 minutes on each side. Remove from heat, place on a plate and allow to rest while warming the flatbreads in the pan. To serve, top the breads with chickpea salad, slices of steak and drizzles of tahini sauce. Scatter with pomegranate seeds (if desired), before folding into a wrap.

VEAL KAPAMA

Ingredients for Pork & Cannellini Bake (right column):
- Zest of 1 lemon
- 3 sprigs of rosemary, leaves picked
- Olive oil
- 1 tsp ground nutmeg
- 1 garlic bulb, broken into cloves
- 200ml white wine
- 200ml chicken stock or water

Cannellini bean bake
- 3 medium leeks
- 1 tbsp butter
- 1 sprig thyme, leaves picked
- 1 x 400g tin chopped tomatoes
- 2 x 400g tins cannellini beans, drained
- 150g crème fraîche
- 100g grated gruyère or cheddar

1 Preheat the oven to 220C/gas 7. Make small incisions in the pork neck fillet and push a smear of butter, a piece of anchovy, some lemon zest and a few rosemary leaves into each one. Drizzle the meat with olive oil, and rub in some nutmeg, salt and lots of pepper. Place the pork in a deep ovenproof pot or a high-sided tray and roast for 30 minutes.
2 Take the pork out the oven and baste with the fat in the tray. Remove pork from tray, then add the garlic. Place pork on top and pour in the wine and stock. Cover tightly with the lid or foil, turn oven down to 180C/gas 4 and return to the oven for another hour.
3 To make the cannellini bake, trim the leeks, chop into chunks, wash and drain. Put a saucepan on a medium heat, add butter, thyme and then the leeks and cook gently, with the lid on, till leeks are very soft but not browned. Add the tomatoes and cook for a few minutes before adding the beans. Fold in the crème fraîche, season and spoon into a ceramic baking dish. Sprinkle over cheese and bake in the oven with the pork for the last 40 minutes of cooking.
4 After the pork has cooked for another hour, remove lid, baste with the pan juices and cook for another 30 minutes to glaze. By this time the meat should be tender, with a ready-made sauce. Pop pork on a big plate, carve into thick chunks and serve with the bean bake.

VEAL KAPAMA
Serves 8
- 4 tbsp extra-virgin olive oil
- 2kg veal shoulder, trimmed and cut into 9cm pieces
- 4 shallots, sliced
- 3 garlic cloves, sliced
- 1-2 cinnamon sticks
- 2-3 fresh bay leaves
- 1 tbsp whole cloves
- 660g tomato passata
- 1kg chantenay or other baby carrots
- Zest and juice of 2 oranges
- Thick Greek-style yoghurt, to serve

Spiced spinach
- 1kg spinach, washed and boiled
- 3 tbsp coarse toasted breadcrumbs
- ½ tbsp chilli flakes

1 Heat oil in a large saucepan over a medium heat and sauté veal for about 8-10 minutes or until browned. Add shallots, garlic, cinnamon, bay and cloves and cook for 10 minutes, stirring, until shallots begin to soften. Season well with sea salt and ground black pepper. Add passata, carrots, orange zest and juice and enough water to just cover the stew. Stir stew well, bring to boil then simmer for 1½-2 hours or until veal is tender and sauce has thickened. Serve with yoghurt and spinach sprinkled with toasted breadcrumbs and chilli flakes.

PORK & CANNELLINI BAKE
Serves 6
- 1 x 1.5kg pork neck fillet joint
- 1 tbsp butter
- 4 anchovy fillets, each one cut into 3 pieces

PORK & CANNELLINI BAKE

KASHMIRI LAMB

BEEF BRAISED IN STOUT

Serves 6-8

- 3kg piece shin of beef, bone in
- Olive oil, for coating beef
- 3 celery hearts
- 6 red shallots, peeled
- 1 garlic bulb, halved across the middle
- 1 tbsp tomato purée
- 1150ml stout
- Small bunch of tarragon, leaves picked
- Mash and winter greens, to serve

1 Preheat the oven to 200C/gas 6. Rub the beef with olive oil, season with salt and black pepper and put in a deep ovenproof pot. Trim the celery hearts, peeling the stringy bits off the outer stalks, then halve them lengthways. Remove the inner leaves and reserve them for later, storing them in ice-cold water in the fridge.
2 Tuck the celery, shallots and garlic around the shin and put the pot in the oven. After 40 minutes, when the shin has coloured, remove from the oven. Lift out the shin and spoon any excess fat out of the pot. Stir in the tomato purée, then replace the shin and pour the stout over. Cover with a lid or foil and return to the oven.
3 Turn the heat down to 180C/gas 4 and cook for 4 hours, or until the meat is soft and coming off the bone. (Check halfway through and if the liquid has reduced too much, add some water from the kettle.) Remove from the oven and uncover. Baste the shin with the pot juices, then bake for 10-15 minutes to reduce the gravy and glaze the meat. Garnish with the reserved celery leaves and the tarragon, and serve with mash and winter greens.

BEEF BRAISED IN STOUT

KASHMIRI LAMB

Serves 4-6

- 4 garlic cloves
- Thumb-sized piece of fresh ginger
- 100ml mustard oil
- 3 green cardamom pods
- 2 cinnamon sticks
- 2-3 blades of mace
- 3 red onions, chopped
- 1 whole leg of lamb, boned and cut into 3cm cubes
- 1½ tbsp ground coriander
- 1 tbsp Kashmiri chilli powder
- 6 tomatoes
- ¼ tsp ground ginger
- ¼ tsp ground fennel seeds

1 In a pestle and mortar, mash garlic and ginger to a paste and put to one side.
2 Heat a saucepan on a medium heat. Add the oil, cardamom, cinnamon, mace and onion and fry gently until golden. Add the lamb. Fry, stirring till browned. Season with salt and add the ginger and garlic paste. Fry, stirring, for 15 minutes, or until everything is dark and aromatic. Add the coriander and chilli powder.
3 Blitz the tomatoes in a blender and add them to the pan. Bring to the boil and simmer for 15-20 minutes until the lamb is cooked through and the tomatoes have reduced to a rich, brown sauce. Add a little water to adjust the consistency if you like. Stir in the ground ginger and fennel seeds and serve with okra and spiced potatoes.

ROAST QUAIL & TABBOULEH

ground black pepper. Before serving, add radishes and combine. Transfer quail to plate, drizzle with marinade and sprinkle over pomegranate seeds. Add tabbouleh and serve.

KENTUCKY-STYLE FRIED CHICKEN

Recipe by Paul Levy
Serves 4
- Vegetable oil, lard or a mixture of both
- One large free-range chicken, jointed into 8 pieces
- Plain flour, seasoned with salt, cayenne and lots of freshly ground black pepper

1 In a large, deep cast-iron frying pan, add the fat until about one-third full. (As always when deep-frying, do not leave the fat unattended and be very careful.) Heat it until a haze rises, or a cube of bread browns in a minute or less. Shake the chicken pieces in seasoned flour in a brown paper bag – the best bags come from Whole Foods, but two greengrocers' bags doubled-up will do. This is not optional – plastic bags make the coating claggy. Shake off any excess flour.
2 Carefully fry the chicken in batches, so as not to crowd the pan. Do the dark meat first, skin-side down, turning. When the chicken is cooked through and perfectly juicy with an all-over golden, crunchy crust, it's done. Drain on kitchen paper and serve quickly – though some prefer it cool, at room temperature.

ROAST QUAIL & TABBOULEH

Serves 4
- 4 quail
- 1 tsp saffron threads
- 1 tbsp za'atar spice mix
- ½ tsp sumac
- 3 tbsp extra-virgin olive oil
- Seeds from ½ pomegranate

Tabbouleh
- 300g bulghur wheat
- Bunch of spring onions, chopped
- Bunch of mint, leaves chopped
- Bunch of dill, leaves and stalks finely chopped
- Bunch of flat-leaf parsley, leaves and stalks finely chopped
- 200ml extra-virgin olive oil
- Juice of 3 lemons
- 12 radishes, trimmed and thinly sliced

1 To start tabbouleh, place the bulghur wheat in a large bowl and cover with water and leave overnight.
2 Place quail in a bowl. Rub saffron, za'atar and sumac over the quail, drizzle with olive oil and season with sea salt and freshly ground black pepper. Cover with clingfilm and refrigerate for at least 30 minutes.
3 Preheat oven to 200C/gas 6. Remove from refrigerator and place quail in a small roasting tin. Pour over marinade ingredients and roast for 40 minutes until golden, basting occasionally with the marinade in bottom of the tin.
4 Meanwhile, to make tabbouleh, drain bulghur wheat in a colander then place in a tea towel and squeeze out any excess water. Place in a large bowl, add spring onions, mint, dill, parsley, olive oil, lemon juice and season generously with sea salt and freshly

KENTUCKY-STYLE FRIED CHICKEN

SPICY PORK CHOPS

SPICY PORK CHOPS

Serves 4

- 4 x 250g pork chops, or 500g pork belly, cut into 4 pieces
- 1 garlic clove, finely chopped
- 1 tsp ground allspice
- Small handful of fresh thyme, torn
- 1 bay leaf
- 3 tbsp olive oil
- 1 tbsp golden rum
- 1 tsp scotch bonnet sauce (see page 164 or use ready-made, Caribbean-style hot sauce)

Avocado, mango & corn salad

- 2 corns on the cob
- 2 avocados, peeled, stoned, sliced
- 1 ripe mango, flesh cubed
- 3 spring onions, peeled and halved lengthways
- Grated zest and juice of 1 lime
- 3 tbsp olive oil

Plantain chips

- 2 plantains
- 1 litre vegetable oil

1 Put pork in a mixing bowl, add garlic and allspice, crumble in thyme and bay leaf, add olive oil, rum and hot sauce. Season with sea salt and black pepper, then stir to coat pork. Marinate for 2–3 hours or, better still, overnight.
2 For avocado, mango and corn salad, barbecue corn for 12–15 minutes, turning, until tender and starting to blacken. (Or cook in a lightly oiled grill pan over a medium heat.) Cut kernels off cob, transfer to a bowl with other ingredients. Stir and season to taste.
3 Remove pork chops from marinade and barbecue for 12–15 minutes, turning once, until evenly cooked. Alternatively, cook in a lightly oiled grill pan over a medium heat.
4 Meanwhile, to make plantain chips, make several incisions in the skin of

PORK TONNATO

plantains. Place in a bowl, cover with boiling water and stand for at least 10 minutes to loosen the skin. Drain, peel and thinly slice into 5mm rounds. Heat oil in a deep saucepan to 180C, or when a cube of bread turns golden and rises to the top. (Never leave hot fat unattended.) Carefully deep-fry plantain in batches for 7–10 minutes, or until tender and golden. Remove plantain from oil with a slotted spoon, drain on absorbent paper and set the oil aside. Season with sea salt and serve immediately with the spicy pork chops and avocado, mango and corn salad.

....

PORK TONNATO

Serves 4

- 375g pork loin fillet
- 4 bay leaves
- 1 tbsp black peppercorns
- 200ml white wine
- 225g tinned tuna, drained
- 3 tbsp capers
- 1 tbsp chopped flat-leaf parsley
- 6 tbsp mayonnaise
- Wild rocket and olive oil, to serve

1 Place the pork in a large saucepan with the bay leaves, peppercorns and white wine, then add enough water to cover the pork. Bring to the boil, then cover, reduce heat to a simmer and poach for 45 minutes, until cooked through and tender. Remove pork from the pan and allow to cool.
2 Make a dressing by combining the tuna with the capers, parsley and mayonnaise. Season to taste. Thinly slice the pork fillet, then arrange on plates. Smear pork slices with tuna mayonnaise, top with wild rocket, drizzle with olive oil and serve.

BRISKET & MELTING BEANS

3 Meanwhile, put the ingredients for the melting beans into a deep pan with 1 litre of water, bring to the boil, then simmer until beans are tender, skimming off any foam that rises to the top.
4 While brisket and beans are cooking, put garlic ingredients in a pan and cook over a very low heat for 1 hour, or until tender. You want the oil to bubble, but never to heat up to frying temperature.
5 After brisket has had another 1½ hours in the oven, take out and remove foil, then return for another 20 minutes.
6 After beans have cooked for 1½ hours, most of the water should have soaked into them. (If too loose, drain off a little water.) Take half the beans out of the pan and mash until smooth, then stir them back into pan with the rest of the beans. Season and keep warm.
7 Slice brisket against the grain into 5mm slices. Season with sea salt and serve on beans with slow-cooked garlic. Scatter with marjoram leaves.

CHICKEN BAKED IN YOGHURT

Serves 4
- Olive oil
- 2 onions, sliced
- 4 chicken breasts (bone on)
- 500ml Greek-style yoghurt
- 2 eggs, beaten
- 2 garlic cloves, sliced
- 2 tbsp plain flour
- 2 tsp dried mint
- 1 tsp ground cumin
- 2 tbsp grated parmesan
- 30g each dry and fresh breadcrumbs

1 Preheat oven to 180C/gas 4. Add some olive oil to a frying pan over a medium heat and sauté the onions till soft, then remove and transfer to a baking dish. In the same pan, sauté chicken breasts for 5 minutes, till golden. Transfer to the dish with the onions. Mix the yoghurt, eggs, garlic, flour, mint and cumin. Season to taste and pour over chicken.
2 Mix parmesan and breadcrumbs, then sprinkle over chicken. Bake for 40-50 minutes till the top is golden-brown and chicken is cooked and tender.

BRISKET & MELTING BEANS

Serves 6
- 1.5-2kg pointy end of brisket, with a thin layer of fat still intact
- Marjoram leaves, to serve

Spice paste
- 6 tbsp American-style mustard
- 1 tbsp worcestershire sauce
- 4 tbsp sweet smoked paprika
- 2 tbsp chilli powder
- 1 tbsp garlic granules
- 1 tsp cayenne pepper

Wrapping mixture
- 125ml honey
- 100g dark brown sugar
- 2 tbsp unsalted butter, melted

Melting beans
- 500g cannellini beans, soaked in water overnight
- 3 garlic cloves, grated
- 1 large white onion, finely diced
- ½ tbsp dried oregano
- 3 tbsp extra-virgin olive oil
- 1 litre chicken stock

Slow-cooked garlic
- 30 garlic cloves, peeled
- 500ml extra-virgin olive oil
- 1 sprig each of rosemary, thyme and sage

1 Preheat oven to 160C/gas 2. Combine spice paste ingredients with 125ml water and freshly ground black pepper. Mix well, spread over brisket and place on a rack over a tray. Roast for 1½ hours.
2 Combine all the wrapping mixture ingredients with 2 tbsp water. Remove the brisket from oven, place on a sheet of foil and brush over the mixture. Wrap meat in foil and return to the oven for another 1½ hours.

CHICKEN BAKED IN YOGHURT

CHILLI LAMB SHANKS

CHILLI LAMB SHANKS

Serves 4

- 2-3 smoked ancho chillies
- Large handful of raisins
- 285ml apple juice
- 4 lamb shanks
- Olive oil
- 3 medium red onions, finely chopped
- 8 garlic cloves, finely sliced
- 2-3 fresh red chillies of your choice, halved and deseeded
- 1 heaped tsp smoked paprika
- 2-3 fresh bay leaves
- 3-4 fresh rosemary sprigs
- 1 x 400g tin tomatoes
- 750ml chicken stock or water
- Dash of red wine vinegar
- Sliced red chillies and garlic (optional)
- Greens and mash, to serve

1 Preheat the oven to full whack. Put the smoked chillies, raisins and apple juice in a bowl then set aside. Put the lamb shanks in a roasting tray then rub them all over with olive oil, sea salt and freshly ground black pepper. Bang them in the hot oven for 20 minutes to brown. Meanwhile, get a casserole-type pan that will fit the 4 shanks quite snugly - about 24cm in diameter and 10cm deep. Put it on a medium heat and add a lug of olive oil. Sweat off the onions, garlic, fresh chilli, paprika, bay leaves and rosemary for about 10 minutes.
2 Once the onions have softened, put the rehydrated chillies and raisins into a food processor or liquidiser, along with any leftover apple juice, then blitz (feel free to sneak in a swig of red wine or bourbon) until you've got a paste. Stir this into your softened onions.
3 By now, the shanks should be browned, so take them out of the oven and turn the temperature down to 140C/gas 1-1½. Add the shanks to the casserole pan along with the tinned tomatoes and stock or water. Stir it all together, then cover and put in the oven to stew for about 2½-3 hours. Top up with water or stock as needed. Once the meat is falling off the bone and the

IRISH STEW

sauce is thick and perfect, take it out of the oven, have a taste and season with salt and pepper and a small swig of vinegar. To give it a kick at the last minute, you can finely chop up a garlic clove and a little bit of fresh chilli then mash it together with a pinch of salt and stir it through for a flavour punch. Serve with steamed greens and mash, or flatbread - whatever you fancy.

IRISH STEW

Serves 4

- 50g butter
- 8 lamb chump chops
- 3 onions, sliced
- 2 carrots, sliced
- 2 large potatoes, sliced
- 6 sprigs fresh thyme
- 3 fresh bay leaves
- 150g pearl barley

1 Preheat the oven to 180C/gas 4. Heat the butter in a large frying pan over a medium heat and brown the chops. Remove from pan then soften onions and carrots for 5 minutes and transfer to a bowl. Add a wineglass of water to the pan, return to the heat and deglaze the pan for 5 minutes, by stirring and scraping the bottom of the pan. Reserve the deglazed liquid.
2 Spread half the potatoes in a layer in a large casserole dish and season well. Add a layer of half the onions and carrots. Add lamb chops, thyme, bay leaves and season again. Add remaining onions and carrots and sprinkle pearl barley on top. Top with remaining potatoes and pour over the deglazed liquid and 500ml water.
3 Cover and bake for 1½-2 hours or until the meat is tender and the potatoes are beginning to crisp up.

BEEF INVOLTINI

PHEASANT STEW

Serves 4

- 2 pheasants
- Plain flour, for coating pheasant joints, plus 50g for the dumplings
- 3 small red onions, chopped
- 2 small carrots, chopped
- 1 celery heart, chopped
- 3 garlic cloves, halved
- 1 tbsp butter
- 200g streaky bacon, cut into lardons
- 6 fresh bay leaves
- 300ml madeira

Chestnut dumplings

- 50g chestnut flour
- 50g suet
- Pinch of baking powder
- 25g ready-cooked chestnuts

1 Cut legs off the pheasants and chop in half at the knee. Cut off breasts and wings in one piece, then chop in half. You'll have 16 pieces in total. Reserve the carcasses. In a bowl, mix a few tbsp of flour with salt and black pepper, and toss in the pheasant to coat. Leave for a while so the flour sticks to the skin.
2 To make a stock, chop the carcasses in half and put them in a pan with a third of the veg and garlic. Add water to cover and bring to the boil. Simmer gently for 1 hour, skimming off any floating bits. Pass through a fine sieve and reserve.
3 Melt butter in a large sauté pan over a medium heat. Add floured pheasant and bacon, then brown slowly on all sides, adding more butter as required. Add bay leaves and remaining veg and garlic. Cook until soft and fragrant. Pour over the madeira and top up with enough stock to just cover the meat. Simmer gently for 45 minutes, adding more stock if the liquid reduces.
4 Preheat oven to 180C/gas 4. Mix all the dumpling ingredients in a bowl, crumbling in the chestnuts. Mix with your fingertips until mixture resembles breadcrumbs, then add salt, pepper, and just enough cold water to bind it all. Dust your hands with flour and roll mixture into brussels sprout-sized balls.
5 Pour stew into an ovenproof pot. Drop in dumplings. Cover with a lid or foil. Bake for 30 minutes until dumplings are fluffy and have soaked up the liquid. Serve with braised red cabbage.

BEEF INVOLTINI

Serves 4

- 500g beef sirloin, cut in 1-1.5cm strips
- 2 tbsp olive oil
- 1 garlic clove, crushed
- ½ tbsp peppercorns in brine, drained
- Pickled green peperoncini
- Roasted red peppers, sliced, or red pepper sauce (below), to serve

Red pepper sauce

- 1 small onion, finely chopped
- 1 garlic clove
- 1 red chilli, sliced
- Olive oil
- 1 x 450g jar roasted red peppers, drained
- ½ tsp sugar
- 1 tsp sherry vinegar
- Small handful of basil leaves

1 For red pepper sauce, sauté the onion, garlic and chilli in olive oil in a frying pan until translucent. Add peppers and heat through, then transfer mixture to a blender. Add sugar, vinegar and basil and blitz until smooth. Season to taste.
2 Mix the beef in a bowl with the oil, garlic and salt and pepper to taste. Cover and refrigerate for 30 minutes.
3 Thread the beef onto medium-length wooden skewers. Heat a large frying pan and sear each skewer for a minute or so on each side. When cooked, place on serving dish. Add green peppercorns to the pan and heat through until they just begin to 'jump' or pop, then pour over the beef involtini. Serve the skewers with the green peperoncini and sliced roasted peppers, or with the red pepper sauce as a dip.

Our wine match

Pair honeyed Domaine Cristia Muscat de Beaumes de Venise with meringue, soft fruits and cream for a simple dessert. Go to page 170 for more details of our great wine offer.

DESSERTS

SWEET SOLUTIONS – HOW TO MAKE YOUR CAKE AND EAT IT TOO

Easy ices (page 130) are a nice way to finish a meal, while soft-centred caramel puddings (page 145) make a grand finale. Jamie's bakewell tart (page 142) impressed world leaders when it was served at 10 Downing Street, but if you just want a slice of cake with a cup of tea, try our Victoria sponge (page 134)

BLOOD ORANGE SORBET

PEACH ICE CREAM

BLOOD ORANGE SORBET

Serves 6-8
- 1 carton blood orange juice
- 1 beaten egg white
- Splash of sugar syrup
- Orange halves, flesh scooped out, to serve

1 Combine blood orange juice, beaten egg white and a splash of sugar syrup in an ice-cream maker and churn according to manufacturer's instructions. Fill scooped-out orange halves with the sorbet and freeze until ready to serve.

PEACH ICE CREAM

Recipe by Paul Levy
Serves 6
- 150g caster sugar
- 500g ripe peaches, peeled, stoned and thickly diced
- 1-2 tbsp brandy or peach schnapps
- 275ml double cream

1 Make a sugar syrup by boiling the sugar with 300ml water for 5 minutes. Pour the hot syrup over the fruit (if you're using an ice-cream maker with its own cooling unit, you can do this in the well of the machine, and leave to cool before switching it on). Add the alcohol, then the cream. Let the mixture cool, then freeze according to your manufacturer's instructions, or freeze the mixture in trays, stirring it at least once when it's half-frozen.
Note You can make a more conventional ice cream with a custard made from 5 egg yolks, well-whisked with 150g caster sugar, to which you add 300ml of almost boiling single cream. Add fruit and alcohol and cool before freezing.

RASPBERRY RIPPLE

Serves 10
- 600ml milk
- 1 vanilla pod, scored lengthways, seeds scraped
- 6 egg yolks
- 150g golden caster sugar
- 600ml double cream
Raspberry ripple
- 225g raspberries, washed
- 100g golden caster sugar

1 Put the milk and vanilla pod and seeds in a heavy-based saucepan and bring almost to the boil. Remove from the heat and infuse for about 20 minutes.
2 To make the ripple, put raspberries, sugar and 1 tbsp of water in a small pan and bring to the boil, then reduce the heat and simmer for a few minutes. Strain through a metal sieve, set aside to cool, then refrigerate until chilled.
3 To make the custard, beat egg yolks with sugar until thick, stir in the vanilla milk and then pour back into the pan. Cook over a low heat, stirring, until it thickens slightly. Don't let it boil or your eggs will scramble. Pour back into the bowl, remove vanilla pod and allow to cool. Whisk the cream to soft peaks and fold into the custard. Freeze in an ice-cream maker according to manufacturer's instructions (see note).
4 As the ice cream finishes churning and is quite soft, stir in the ripple. Transfer to a container and freeze for another hour or so. Serve in cones, sandwiched between wafers or with some shortbread.
Note If you don't have an ice-cream maker, set your freezer to maximum, or fast-freeze about an hour before you intend to use it. When you've made the ice cream mixture, pour it into a shallow, non-metal container, cover and freeze for 3 hours, until just frozen. Remove container and mash everything with a fork to break down the ice crystals, quickly, so the ice cream doesn't melt. Freeze again for 2 hours, then mash as before. Fold in the ripple, then freeze for another 2 hours, or until firm.

CHOCOLATE HALVA ICE CREAM

Recipe by Greg Malouf, Momo, Melbourne, Australia

Halva is a sesame-based confectionary that's popular throughout the Middle East. It's not overly sweet, so works brilliantly in ice cream. It's available from delicatessens and supermarkets.

Makes 1.8 litres

- 50g cocoa powder, preferably Dutch-process
- 100g dark chocolate, broken into small pieces
- 1 litre cream
- 500ml full-cream milk
- 12 egg yolks
- 250g caster sugar
- 120g plain or chocolate halva

1 Place the cocoa and chocolate in a large mixing bowl. Combine the cream and milk in a heavy-based saucepan and bring to a gentle simmer. Remove from the heat. In another large bowl, whisk the egg yolks with the sugar until thick and creamy. Gradually pour in the hot milk, whisking continuously. Return the mixture to the pan and cook gently over a medium heat, stirring frequently, until it thickens and coats the back of a spoon. Remove from the heat and pour the hot custard over the cocoa powder and chocolate. Stir until the mixture is very smooth. Allow to cool – ideally over a bowl of ice – then pour into an ice-cream machine and churn according to manufacturer's instructions. (You may need to churn in two batches depending on the size of your machine.)
2 While the ice cream is churning, using a mortar and pestle, crush the halva to large crumbs. At the very end of the churning time, add the halva and churn in briefly. Transfer ice cream to a plastic container and freeze until needed.

CRANBERRY GALETTE

CRANBERRY GALETTE

Serves 6

- 375g ready-made sweet pastry
- 2 punnets of cranberries, or 400g frozen cranberries, defrosted
- 100g golden caster sugar
- Zest of 2 clementines
- Double cream, for brushing
- 2 tbsp demerara sugar

1 Preheat an oven to 180C/gas 4. Roll the sweet pastry into a rough circle, about 5mm thick. Carefully put the pastry onto a lined baking sheet. Mix the cranberries with the golden caster sugar and the clementine zest, then set them aside for 5 minutes to marinate.
2 Pile the fruit and sugar mixture into the middle of the pastry, leaving an edge of a couple of inches. Gently bring the pastry edge up around the berries, pinching it in as you go. Brush the pastry with cream, then sprinkle with demerara sugar. Bake for 25–30 minutes, until the pastry is golden and cooked through and the berries are caramelising.

CHOCOLATE CHERRY CAKE

VICTORIA SANDWICH
Serves 8
- 200g very soft unsalted butter, plus extra for greasing
- 200g golden caster sugar
- 4 large eggs
- 200g self-raising flour, plus extra for dusting
- 1 rounded tsp baking powder
- 2 tbsp rosewater, plus a splash extra
- Caster sugar, for dusting

Filling
- 250ml double cream
- 1 vanilla pod, split, seeds scraped
- 1 dessertspoon golden caster sugar
- 4 tbsp raspberry jam (see page 163)
- 120g raspberries, squashed slightly

1 Preheat the oven to 180C/gas 4. Grease two 20cm sandwich tins, line the base of each tin with greaseproof paper and dust sides lightly with flour. Beat the butter with the sugar till light and fluffy. Add the eggs one at a time, beating in each before adding the next, then fold in the flour, baking powder and rosewater. Divide mixture between the tins, spreading it evenly with a spatula. Bake for 20 minutes, until lightly golden-brown. Stick a wooden skewer into the centre of the cake: if it comes out clean, it's done; if it's sticky, return the cake to the oven for a few minutes. Let cakes cool slightly then turn out onto a rack to cool completely.
2 Meanwhile, lightly whip your cream with the vanilla seeds, sugar and a splash of rosewater until soft peaks form. Pick your prettiest cake and set aside. Take the other one and place it on your serving plate. Trim the top to make it flat, then spread with jam, followed by cream. Scatter over some raspberries, top with the other cake and dust with caster sugar.

CHOCOLATE CHERRY CAKE
Serves 8-10
- 200g 70%-cocoa chocolate, broken
- 150g unsalted butter, cubed
- 50g ground almonds
- 100g self-raising flour
- 4 large eggs
- 100g caster sugar
- 3 tbsp cherry jam
- Fresh cherries, to serve

1 Preheat an oven to 180C/gas 4. Place the broken chocolate and cubed butter in a bowl over a pan of simmering water.

Leave until melted, then cool slightly and stir in the ground almonds and flour. In a separate bowl, whisk the eggs with the caster sugar for 5 minutes, then fold the egg mixture into the chocolate mixture.
2 Line a 20cm springform cake tin with baking paper, then spoon in the cake batter. Bake for 20–25 minutes, until set but still slightly soft in the centre. Remove the cake from the oven and allow to cool for a little while in the tin, then transfer to a wire rack to cool further. You can serve this at room temperature or still slightly warm. Spread with cherry jam while warm and top with fresh cherries before serving.

LEMON MOUSSE

KARYDOPITA

LEMON MOUSSE

Serves 6
- 185g caster sugar
- 3 large eggs, separated
- Juice and grated zest of 2 lemons
- 3 tsp powdered gelatine
- 300ml double cream
- Grated dark chocolate, to serve

1 Whisk the sugar and egg yolks until pale and thick. Whisk in the lemon juice and zest. In a small bowl, combine 100ml boiling water with the gelatine, whisk to dissolve, then stir into the yolk mixture. In another bowl, beat the cream to soft peaks, then fold into the yolk mixture. In yet another bowl, whisk the egg whites until stiff peaks form and fold into the cream mixture. Pour into a large dish (or 6 small ones), cover with clingfilm and chill overnight. Sprinkle with chocolate.

KARYDOPITA

Recipe from Agnanti restaurant, Glossa, Greece
- 100g unsalted butter
- 4 eggs, separated
- 100g caster sugar
- 200g walnuts, finely chopped
- 75ml brandy
- 200g fine semolina
- 1 tsp baking powder
- 1 tsp ground cinnamon
- Grated zest of 1 orange
- 150ml orange juice

Syrup
- 300ml water
- 125g granulated sugar
- 1 small cinnamon stick
- 2 strips lemon zest

1 Beat the butter, egg yolks and sugar together till light and fluffy. Pound half the walnuts in a pestle and mortar till finely ground, and add to the butter mix with the brandy and remaining walnuts. 2 Combine the semolina, baking powder, cinnamon and orange zest in a bowl. In another bowl, whisk the egg whites till stiff then fold in the semolina mixture and orange juice. Fold all this into butter mixture. 3 Heat oven to 180C/gas 4. Grease a 20cm x 25cm baking dish, then add in cake batter. Bake for about 35-40 minutes or until a skewer inserted into middle of the cake comes out clean. Remove from oven, prick the surface all over with a fork and allow to cool. 4 Combine all the syrup ingredients in a pan, bring to the boil, then simmer for 10 minutes. Discard the cinnamon stick and lemon zest, then pour the hot syrup over the cooled cake. Allow to cool again before cutting and serving.

TIRAMISU

LEMON & POPPY SEED CAKE

Serves 6-8
- 250g caster sugar
- 3 large eggs
- 250g self-raising flour
- 200ml melted butter
- Grated zest of 1 lemon
- 2 tbsp poppy seeds

Filling
- 175ml double cream
- 2 tbsp icing sugar

Icing
- 100g icing sugar
- 1 lemon
- 1 tbsp poppy seeds, optional

1 Preheat oven to 180C/gas 4. Beat the caster sugar with the eggs until thick and pale. Add the self-raising flour, melted butter, grated lemon zest and poppy seeds. Mix until smooth. Spoon the batter into a 23cm cake tin and bake for 30-40 minutes, depending on your oven. When it's golden and a skewer inserted into the centre comes out clean, it's cooked. Leave to cool, then split the cake in half horizontally.
2 For the filling, whisk the double cream with 2 tbsp icing sugar to soft peaks. Spread thickly over the bottom half of the cake. For the icing, mix 100g icing sugar with the juice of ½ lemon, and slice the other lemon half very thinly. Place the other half of the cake on top of the cream, then spread it with icing and top with the lemon slices. If you like, you can scatter more poppy seeds over the top of the cake. This cake is best eaten the day it's made.

TIRAMISU

Serves 8
- 6 large eggs, separated
- 230g icing sugar
- 500g mascarpone
- 250ml double cream
- 250ml strong black coffee, cooled
- 250ml Tia Maria
- 20 sponge fingers
- Cocoa, for dusting

1 Whisk the egg yolks and icing sugar till pale and thick. Fold in the mascarpone. Whisk the cream in another bowl until soft peaks form. Fold the cream into the mascarpone mixture with a spatula until well combined. In another bowl, whisk the egg whites to soft peaks and fold into the mascarpone mixture.
2 Combine the coffee and Tia Maria in a bowl. Spoon a layer of the mascarpone mixture into 8 glasses. Dip the sponge fingers into the coffee mixture and them crumble them into the glasses, pressing down to form a layer of biscuit. Repeat the process with the remaining mascarpone mixture and sponge fingers. Refrigerate for a few hours or overnight. Dust with cocoa and serve.

LEMON & POPPY SEED CAKE

PISTACHIO TART

Quick fix

Pan-fry pineapple or banana slices with brown sugar and butter until caramelised, drizzle in golden rum, then serve with crème fraîche. Toast slices of raisin bread or brioche and top with poached fruit and honey. Crumble macaroons with orange zest and spoon into stoned peach halves before roasting, or core whole apples and fill with currants, nuts and stem ginger before baking. Stir smashed meringues with berries and whipped cream, or crumble shortbread over ice cream. Freeze homemade lemon cordial or sweet espresso, then scrape with a fork to make granita. Make ice cubes from fruit juice and herbs like basil or mint, then let them melt over a fruit salad and add a splash of dessert wine before serving.

GOOSEBERRY FOOL & GARIBALDIS

PISTACHIO TART

Serves 8

- 375g ready-made sweet pastry
- 200g candied fruit, chopped
- Good splash of brandy
- 150g light brown sugar
- 150g unsalted butter, softened
- 3 eggs
- 150g ground almonds,
- 50g self-raising flour
- 100g pistachios

1 Preheat the oven to 180C/gas 4. Roll out pastry to line a 24cm tart tin. Cover with baking paper, weight with rice and bake for 10 minutes. Lift out the paper and rice and bake for another 5 minutes. 2 Mix all ingredients except pistachios. Spread mixture into the tart shell, then sprinkle over the nuts. Bake for 25–30 minutes, till set and golden. Serve warm.

GOOSEBERRY FOOL & GARIBALDIS

Serves 8

- 800g gooseberries
- 200g golden caster sugar
- 2 vanilla pods, scored lengthways, seeds scraped
- 500ml double cream
- 500ml plain yoghurt

Garibaldi biscuits (makes 30)

- 150g unsalted butter
- 150g icing sugar
- 200g plain flour
- 2 eggs
- 200g currants or dried blueberries

1 Preheat the oven to 180C/gas 4. In a food processor, blitz the butter, icing sugar and flour until smooth, then add the eggs and blitz again. Remove to a bowl and fold in the currants. Bring the dough into a ball and roll into a long flat sausage shape, wrap in clingfilm and put into the fridge to chill and firm up. 2 Meanwhile, put the gooseberries, sugar, vanilla seeds and pods in a saucepan over a medium heat. Stew for 10 minutes, until fruit has softened. 3 Allow berries to cool while you bake the garibaldis. Remove dough from fridge and cut off 5mm slices. Put onto a tray lined with baking paper and bake for 10 minutes, until golden-brown. 4 Meanwhile, whip the cream to soft peaks and fold through the yoghurt. Once the berries have cooled, fold most of them through the cream and spoon into bowls. Spoon over the remaining gooseberries. Serve the fool with a couple of garibaldi biscuits.

SOUFFLE GLACE AUX MARRONS

BAKEWELL TART

Serves 8

- Knob of butter
- 10-12 tbsp good-quality jam
- 8 ginger nut biscuits, crushed finely
- Clotted cream or custard, to serve

Pastry

- 250g plain flour, plus extra for dusting
- 50g icing sugar
- 125g good-quality cold butter, cubed
- Zest of ½ lemon
- 1 large egg, beaten
- Splash of milk

Frangipane

- 250g blanched whole almonds, ground
- 50g plain flour
- 1 vanilla pod, halved, seeds scraped
- 250g unsalted butter, cubed
- 250g caster sugar
- 3 large eggs, lightly beaten

1 To make pastry, sieve flour, then icing sugar, onto a clean surface. With fingers, rub butter into flour and sugar till fine and crumbly. Grate over lemon zest. Make a well and tip in egg and milk. Use a fork to bring it together, then use your hands to gently work it until you have a ball of dough. Don't over-handle it. Sprinkle flour over work surface, pat dough into a round, flour lightly, wrap in clingfilm and refrigerate for 30 minutes.
2 Grease a loose-bottomed 26cm-round tart tin. Roll out the pastry on a floured surface. Line the tin with the pastry. Prick with a fork, then freeze for an hour.
3 Make frangipane by blitzing butter, sugar and vanilla seeds until creamy in a food processor, then add the almonds, flour and eggs and blitz till smooth. Transfer to a bowl and chill for 30 minutes.
4 Preheat oven to 180C/gas 4. Line pastry case with baking paper, fill with rice and blind bake 10 minutes. Remove the rice and paper and return to oven for 6-7 minutes, till light golden.
5 Spoon jam into tart case and spread evenly. Spread frangipane over jam, then scatter over a quarter of the ginger nut crumbs. Place tart in oven, with a baking tray on the shelf below to catch any spills, then bake for 40-45 minutes. Once cooked and golden brown, remove from oven and let cool a little. Scatter over remaining ginger crumbs, then serve warm, with clotted cream or custard.

SOUFFLE GLACE AUX MARRONS

Recipe by Bernard Perrier, Hotel du Midi, Lamastre, France

Serves 4

- 250ml full-fat milk
- 4 large egg yolks
- 75g caster sugar
- 250g chestnut purée
- 500ml crème fraîche
- 125g icing sugar, sifted

1 Put the milk in a saucepan over a low heat, simmer till nearly boiling then take off the heat. Meanwhile, whisk the egg yolks and sugar in a large bowl until the mixture is very pale. Whisk in a little milk, then slowly whisk in the rest. Pour into the pan over a low heat, stirring constantly, till it thickens and coats the back of a wooden spoon. Remove from the heat and place the saucepan in a bowl of cold water that reaches halfway up its side. When cold, add the chestnut purée, stirring to combine.
2 Combine the crème fraîche and icing sugar in a bowl and whisk until the mixture is firmly whipped. Gently fold into the chestnut mixture.
3 Place 8cm-high strips of greaseproof paper around four 6cm-diameter, 4cm-deep ramekins; secure with string.
4 Pour soufflé mix into an ice-cream machine and freeze according to manufacturer's instructions. Place the ramekins on a tray and divide the mixture between them, then place the ramekins in the freezer for 3 hours.
5 To serve, remove the ramekins from the freezer 15 minutes before you need them. Remove the greaseproof paper, then clean the edges of the ramekins.

APPLE TART & LAVENDER CREAM

APPLE TART & LAVENDER CREAM

If you can't find any lavender flowers for the cream, don't worry, just try and get some fragrant honey to add a little bit of floral flavour.

Serves 10-12

- 6 bramley apples
- 40g butter
- 500g ready-made puff pastry
- 1 egg
- 4 tbsp caster sugar
- Icing sugar, for dusting

Lavender cream

- 1 tbsp lavender honey
- 400g crème fraîche or double cream
- 1 tbsp fresh lavender flowers

1 Peel, core and roughly chop 2 apples. Place in a saucepan with the butter and cook over moderate heat for 20 minutes, or until soft and slightly puréed. Allow to cool. Peel, core and quarter remaining apples, then cut into thin slices.

2 Preheat the oven to 200C/gas 6. Roll the pastry out to 3mm thick then cut out a 30cm-diameter circle. Place on lightly greased baking tray and score an inner circle 1½cm from the pastry edge to prevent rising.

3 Spread the purée over the inner circle of the base and top with the remaining apple slices in concentric circles. Beat the egg with 1 tbsp water and use to brush the pastry edge. Sprinkle tart with 1 tbsp sugar, then bake for 20 minutes.

4 While the tart is cooking, heat 3 tbsp sugar and 3 tbsp water over a medium heat in a small saucepan until the sugar dissolves and mixture reduces a little and becomes syrupy.

5 For the lavender cream, combine the honey and crème fraîche or whipped cream in a bowl. Just before serving, sprinkle with the lavender flowers.

6 Remove tart from oven, brush with sugar syrup, then turn the oven up to 220C/gas 7 and cook for a further 10 minutes or until top begins to caramelise. Remove from oven and leave to cool. Dust with icing sugar and serve with lavender cream.

MOELLEUX CARAMEL

MOELLEUX CARAMEL

Recipe by Stéphane Reynaud

To make these soft caramel puddings, you'll need six 1-cup aluminium foil moulds, available from supermarkets.

Serves 6

- 150g granulated sugar
- 80ml double cream
- 100g salted butter
- 140g plain flour, sifted
- 4 eggs, lightly beaten
- Vegetable oil for greasing moulds

Chestnut cream

- 20ml double cream
- 250g chestnut purée

1 Make a caramel by combining sugar and 2 tbsp cold water in a saucepan over a medium heat. When the caramel has turned a beautiful golden colour, add 80ml cream and the butter, combine well, then allow to cool. Add the flour and eggs and mix well.

2 Preheat the oven to 180C/gas 4. Lightly grease the 6 moulds and pour in the caramel mixture. Bake in the oven for 7 minutes.

3 For the chestnut cream, beat the cream till thickened, then fold the chestnut purée into the cream and transfer to a serving bowl.

4 When cooked, turn the caramel cakes out onto plates and serve with a good dollop of chestnut cream.

TROPICAL FRUIT PAVLOVA

CHERRY PIE

Serves 8

- Butter, for greasing
- 600g pitted cherries
- Juice and zest of 1 lemon
- 1 tbsp plain flour
- 1½ tbsp cornflour
- 150g caster sugar
- 1 tsp vanilla extract
- 30g unsalted butter, diced
- Egg wash (1 egg beaten with 6 tbsp milk)

Pastry

- 500g plain flour
- 255g unsalted chilled butter, diced
- 150g icing sugar
- 6 egg yolks

1 For pastry, place flour, butter and icing sugar in a food processor and process until mixture resembles breadcrumbs. Add egg yolks, one at a time, then gradually add 1–2 tablespoons of chilled water until mixture forms a ball. Knead on a floured surface for 30 seconds. Divide in half, wrap each half in clingfilm and then refrigerate for at least 1 hour.
2 Lightly grease a 22cm (across the top) round metal or glass pie dish with melted butter. Remove dough from refrigerator and roll out one piece on a lightly floured surface into a 30cm circle, about 5-7mm thick. Drape dough over rolling pin and then carefully unroll it over the dish, gently pressing into the bottom and sides. Cut off excess pastry, leaving a 2.5cm overhang around the edge of the pie dish. Chill while you prepare the filling.
3 For filling, place cherries, lemon juice and zest, flour, cornflour, sugar and vanilla extract in a bowl and mix well. Leave to stand uncovered at room temperature for 10 minutes.
4 Remove pie dish from fridge and spoon the filling evenly into the pastry shell. Dot the top with diced butter.
5 Preheat oven to 200C/gas 6. Roll out remaining pastry as before. Brush the edge with egg wash then drape dough over rolling pin and place it over the pie. Trim off excess from rim and press edges together to seal. Cut 3 slashes in top, brush with egg wash and bake for 10 minutes. Lower heat to 180C/gas 4 and bake for a further 40 minutes, till top is golden. Allow to cool before serving.

TROPICAL FRUIT PAVLOVA

Serves 8

- 6 egg whites
- 300g caster sugar
- 1 tsp white vinegar
- 300ml double cream, whipped
- Flesh of ½ pineapple, chopped
- 2 tamarillos, peeled and quartered
- 2 bananas, peeled and sliced
- Pulp of 8 passion fruit
- Runny honey, to serve

1 Preheat oven to 150C/gas 2. Grease a 24cm baking tray, line with baking paper. Using an electric beater, whisk the egg whites with a pinch of salt till soft peaks form, then gradually add the sugar till incorporated and mixture is glossy and forms firm peaks. Fold in the vinegar, then spoon the mixture onto a baking tray. Make a slight well in the centre, then bake for 1 hour. When meringue is crisp, turn off oven and leave till cold.
2 When meringue is cold, spread with whipped cream. Top with cut fruit and passion-fruit pulp. Drizzle with honey.

KEY LIME PIE

KEY LIME PIE

Serves 10

- 4 egg yolks
- 400ml condensed milk
- 6 tbsp fresh lime juice (about 5 limes' worth)
- 200ml double cream
- Lime zest (optional), to serve

Crust

- 12 digestive biscuits
- 45g caster sugar
- 135g melted unsalted butter

1 Preheat oven to 175C/gas 3. For the pie crust, lightly grease a 22cm (across the top) metal or glass pie dish with a little of the melted butter. Blend digestive biscuits, caster sugar and remaining melted butter in a food processor until the mixture resembles breadcrumbs. Transfer to pie dish and spread over the bottom and up the sides, firmly pressing the mixture down. Bake for 10 minutes, or until lightly browned. Remove from oven and place dish on a wire rack to cool.

2 For the filling, whisk the egg yolks in a bowl. Gradually whisk in condensed milk until smooth. Mix in lime juice, then pour filling into pie crust and level over with the back of a spoon.

3 Return to the oven for 15 minutes then place on a wire rack to cool. Refrigerate for 6 hours or overnight.

4 To serve, whip the cream until it just holds stiff peaks. Add dollops of cream to the top of the pie, and grate over some lime zest, if you'd like some extra zing.

COURGETTE & CARDAMOM CAKE

COURGETTE & CARDAMOM CAKE

Serves 6-8

- 1 large courgette, grated
- 100g caster sugar
- 175g butter, plus extra for greasing
- 100g honey
- 3 eggs, beaten
- 1 heaped tsp green cardamom pods, seeds removed and crushed
- Zest and juice of 2 limes
- 325g self-raising flour
- 75g ground almonds
- 3 tbsp Greek yoghurt
- 100g icing sugar
- 100g cream cheese

1 Preheat oven to 180C/gas 4. Grease a 900g loaf tin with butter. Spread the courgette on kitchen paper to soak up moisture. Cream the sugar and 100g butter till pale, then beat in the honey and eggs. Fold in the cardamom seeds, zest and juice of 1 lime, flour, courgette and almonds. Stir in the yoghurt, then pour the mixture into the loaf tin.

2 Bake for about 1 hour and 20 minutes, till golden and cooked through. Check the cake after 1 hour, though it may need longer depending on your oven; when a skewer inserted into the centre comes out clean, the cake is done. Remove from oven to cool in the tin.

3 Beat the icing sugar with remaining butter till smooth. Mix in cream cheese and remaining lime juice. Ice cake and sprinkle over remaining zest.

STRAWBERRY SHORTCAKE

STICKY DOUBLE GINGER CAKE

It's easy to make this cake in a food processor but if you're doing it by hand you'll need to chop your ginger very finely and make sure you cream your sugars and butter really well. If you like, you can stab the cake with a skewer and then douse it with rum.

Serves 8-10

- 8 pieces of stem ginger in syrup, drained, reserving 4 tbsp syrup
- 150g butter
- 200g golden syrup
- 100g dark muscovado sugar
- 250g self-raising flour
- 1 tbsp ground ginger
- 1 tsp ground cinnamon
- 2 eggs
- 200ml milk
- 100g light muscovado sugar

1 Preheat the oven to 180C/gas 4. In a food processor, pulse the pieces of stem ginger until roughly chopped. Transfer to a large mixing bowl and set aside. Next throw in the butter, golden syrup, dark muscovado sugar and 4 tbsp of ginger syrup. Blitz until pale and creamy, then add the flour and spices and blitz again. Add the eggs and milk and whiz it all up once more. Pour the cake mixture into the bowl with the chopped ginger and mix well.
2 Grease and line a 20cm-round loose-bottomed cake tin or a loaf tin measuring 20cm x 10cm with baking parchment. Pour in your cake mixture, sprinkle over the light muscovado sugar and bake until a skewer inserted into the centre comes out clean. Check it at 50 minutes; it may need up to 20 minutes more, depending on your oven. If the cake is browning too much, cover the top with foil. When cooked, remove from the oven and let stand in the tin before turning out onto a wire rack to finish cooling before cutting.

STRAWBERRY SHORTCAKE

Serves 6

- A little melted butter
- 270g plain flour, plus extra
- 1 tbsp baking powder
- 300ml thick cream, plus extra for brushing

Filling

- 450g strawberries, sliced
- 2 tbsp granulated sugar
- 1 tbsp icing sugar
- 1 tsp vanilla extract
- 250ml double cream

1 Preheat the oven to 220C/gas 7 and grease a baking sheet with butter.
2 Sift together flour, baking powder and ½ tsp salt into a bowl. Add cream and mix until a dough just forms. Gather dough into a ball and gently knead 6 times on a lightly floured surface.
3 Pat dough into a 25cm circle, about 1-1.5cm thick, on a lightly floured surface. Cut out 4 rounds with a lightly floured 7.5cm cutter and place onto a baking sheet. Gather any scraps of dough, pat out again and cut out remaining 2 rounds.
4 Brush the tops of the shortcakes with some cream and bake for 15-20 minutes until a pale golden colour. Transfer to a rack and leave to cool.
5 Gently mash the strawberries in a bowl with the sugar, icing sugar and vanilla extract. In another bowl, beat cream until it's just holding soft peaks.
6 Cut the shortcakes in half. Arrange the bottom halves on plates, dollop some cream over the top, spoon strawberry mixture over, then cover with shortcake tops.

STICKY DOUBLE GINGER CAKE

Our wine match
Use sugarcubes and this delicious
Moutard Champagne in a classic
cocktail. To buy this lovely bubbly,
go to page 170 and read the details
of our great wine club offer.

DRINKS & SAUCES

YOU'LL NEVER GO THIRSTY, OR HAVE A BARE CUPBOARD, AGAIN

If you're celebrating, you'll want to make a bellini (page 154) but if you're hot you might prefer an icy frappé (page 159). If you're looking for basics, you will find recipes for a classic béchamel (160), a meat ragù (page 164), herby mayo (165) or an easy caesar salad dressing (page 163) useful

PINA COLADA

POMEGRANATE BELLINI

PINA COLADA
Serves 1

Combine 1 shot of white rum, 1 shot of golden rum, 3 shots of pineapple juice and 2 tbsp of coconut cream with ice in cocktail shaker. Shake and strain into glass filled with ice. Garnish with a pineapple slice and a cocktail cherry.

POMEGRANATE BELLINI

Sprinkle some pomegranate seeds in a champagne flute, pour in a dash of Chambord and top up with prosecco.

SPICED CIDER
Serves 8

- 1.5 litre cider
- 500ml apple juice
- 2 star anise
- 1 cinnamon stick
- Freshly grated nutmeg
- 4 tbsp light brown sugar
- Strips of zest from 2 oranges
- Dark rum
- Cinnamon sticks, to serve

1 Pour the cider and apple juice into a medium pan, add the star anise, cinnamon stick, a good grating of nutmeg, light brown sugar and the orange zest. Simmer on a low heat for 15 minutes, but don't let it boil. Finish with a good splash of dark rum and serve in glasses or mugs, garnished with sticks of cinnamon.

CHOCOLATE & PEANUT BUTTER MILKSHAKE
Serves 4

- 600ml semi-skimmed milk
- 4 tbsp chocolate ice cream
- 2 tbsp smooth peanut butter
- 4 tbsp vanilla ice cream

1 Blitz the milk, chocolate ice cream and peanut butter in a blender. Pour into glasses, top with a scoop of vanilla ice cream and serve.

BOURBON SOUR
Serves 1

Rub cut lemon around the top of glass, then twist the glass upside down in saucer of sugar. Shake 1 shot of bourbon, 1 teaspoon of sugar syrup and the juice of ½ lemon in a cocktail shaker with ice. Strain into a glass with cracked ice. Garnish with lemon zest.

VELVET KISS
Serves 1

Combine 1 shot of gin, 1 shot of crème de bananes, 1 shot of cream, 2 shots of pineapple juice, and a dash of grenadine with ice in a cocktail shaker. Shake and strain into a chilled cocktail glass.

VICTOR
Serves 1

Combine 1 shot of gin, 1 shot of brandy, 1 shot of sweet vermouth with some ice in a cocktail shaker. Shake and strain into a chilled cocktail glass.

KUMQUAT BRANDY
Makes 1 bottle

- 2 handfuls of kumquats
- 75g golden caster sugar
- 1 vanilla pod, split and seeds scraped
- 750ml brandy

1 Wash the kumquats and prick each with a needle. Put in a sterilised jar with the sugar and vanilla pod and seeds, then pour in the brandy. Give it a shake, and leave to infuse for a few weeks, shaking now and then. When nicely infused, strain and re-bottle the brandy.

DANDELION & BURDOCK

Good health food shops sell both dandelion and burdock powder.

Make 1.5 litres of syrup

- 2 tbsp dandelion root powder
- 2 tbsp burdock root powder
- 2 star anise
- Thumb-sized piece of ginger, peeled and chopped into rounds
- 1 orange
- 1 lemon
- 2 tbsp black treacle
- 1kg golden caster sugar
- Ice, lemons and soda water, to serve

1 Put 1.5 litres of water into a pan with the root powders, star anise and ginger. Peel in the zest of the orange and lemon, and squeeze in the juice of both. Bring to the boil and allow to simmer for about 20 minutes. Strain through a fine sieve, muslin, or even a clean tea towel. Clean the pan, add the mixture, put it back onto a medium heat and add the treacle and sugar. Heat, stirring, till the sugar dissolves, then let cool. Transfer to clean bottles, and store in the fridge. This should keep for a few months.
2 Add ice and lemon to glasses, then mix 1 part syrup to 3 parts soda water.

DANDELION & BURDOCK

TURBO PICK-ME-UP SMOOTHIE

Serves 4

- 200g frozen blueberries
- 500ml apple juice
- 250g good-quality plain yoghurt
- 2 bananas
- Thumb-sized piece of ginger, peeled
- Juice of 2 oranges
- 1 big tsp honey
- 1 handful of rolled oats (optional)

1 Pop all the ingredients into a blender. Blitz it all up until lovely and smooth then divide between glasses and serve. If you have any left over, turn it into a simple sorbet. Pour it into a bowl and freeze for 40 minutes. Once it's a bit frozen, mix it with a fork to make it fluffy, then put it in the freezer until it's frozen but easy to scoop into bowls.

LYCHEE FIZZ

Serves 6-8

Blend ½ bottle prosecco, 400g tinned lychees, lime juice, mint and ice, pour into flutes and top up with prosecco.

SEX ON THE BEACH

Serves 1

Shake 1 shot of vodka, 1 shot of peach brandy and 3 shots each of cranberry and pineapple juice with ice in cocktail shaker. Strain into a chilled glass with ice.

SAZERAC

Serves 1

Muddle 1 shot of rye whiskey and ½ teaspoon of sugar in a chilled tumbler.

Add ice cubes, 1 shot of Pernod and a dash of Angostura bitters. Stir and garnish with lemon peel.

YELLOW BIRD

Serves 1

Place 1 shot of golden rum, 1 shot of Cointreau, 1 shot of Galliano and juice of ½ lime with crushed ice in a blender. Blend until smooth and pour into a chilled cocktail glass.

SILK STOCKINGS

Serves 1

Combine 1 shot of white tequila, 1 shot of white crème de cacao, 1 shot of cream and a dash of grenadine with ice in a cocktail shaker. Shake and strain into a chilled cocktail glass and sprinkle with ground cinnamon.

PASSION FRUIT CAIPIRINHA

HURRICANE OLIVER

Makes 6 big glasses
- Juice of 6 blood oranges or 6 regular oranges
- Juice of 4 limes
- 300ml pineapple juice
- 50ml grenadine
- 4 passion fruit
- Crushed ice, to serve
- 6 x 50ml shots dark rum

1 Pour the orange, lime and pineapple juices in a big jug with the grenadine. Halve your passion fruits and scoop the seeds into the jug. Give everything a good stir then fill 6 tall glasses with crushed ice. Add a generous shot of dark rum to each glass then top up with your hurricane mix.

BETWEEN THE SHEETS

Serves 1
Shake 1 shot of brandy, 1 shot of white rum, 1 shot of white curaçao and juice of ½ lime with ice in a cocktail shaker. Strain into a chilled cocktail glass. Garnish with a twist of lime.

PASSION FRUIT CAIPIRINHA

Serves 1
- ½ a lime
- 1 tbsp brown sugar
- Pulp of 1 passion fruit
- 1 large shot of cachaça

1 Cut your lime into wedges and place in a tumbler with the brown sugar, then pound together with a wooden spoon so that the sugar dissolves. Stir in the passion fruit. Top with crushed ice and pour over a large shot of cachaça.

MINT JULEP

Serves 1
Muddle 1 teaspon of sugar and 6 sprigs of mint with dash of water in a tumbler.

Stir in 1 shot of bourbon and crushed ice. Garnish with mint sprigs.

CHILLI VODKA

Infusing vodka is a fantastic way to make cocktails more interesting. Use a split vanilla pod, blackcurrants, lemon peel - start experimenting with your favourite flavours.
- 3 fresh red chillies
- 3 fresh yellow chillies
- 1 bottle of vodka

1 Prick chillies a few times, then warm them in a pan over a low heat with half the vodka. After a few minutes take the pan off the heat, let the vodka cool then pour it into the bottle. Pop as many chillies as you can fit in there. Store the bottle in the freezer. The longer you leave it, the more fiery it will be!

HOT CAIPIROSKA

Serves 2
- Chilli salt (see page 160)
- 4 shots chilli vodka (see left)
- Small bunch of mint, leaves picked
- 2 tbsp caster sugar
- 3 limes, quartered
- A few large handfuls of crushed ice

1 Place some chilli salt in a thin layer on a small plate. Put the vodka, mint leaves, sugar and lime wedges, reserving one, into a jug. Use the end of a rolling pin to muddle everything together till the flavours have mingled and the sugar has dissolved. Run the reserved lime wedge around the rims of 2 glasses then dip each into the salt to lightly coat the rims (coat half the glass rim, if you prefer). Fill each halfway with crushed ice then pour in your muddled lime and vodka mixture.

RASPBERRY & ROSE SYRUP

SEA BREEZE;
COSMOPOLITAN

RASPBERRY & ROSE SYRUP

Makes about 850ml

- 500g raspberries, washed
- 400g golden caster sugar
- 2 tbsp good rose extract, or lots of rose petals, washed

1 In a bowl, squash the raspberries, sugar and rose extract (or petals) until mushy, then mix in 250ml just-boiled water. To make a fresh syrup, strain through a sieve, pressing with a spoon to get out all the juice, into a jug or bottle. Serve chilled as a drink with sparkling water and ice cubes. For a longer-lasting syrup, boil the squished berries, sugar, rose extract or petals and water, then simmer for 3 minutes, skimming away any foam. Strain through a sieve, transfer to a bottle and keep in the fridge for up to two weeks.

SEA BREEZE

Serves 1

Combine 1 shot of vodka, 2 shots of grapefruit juice and 3 shots of cranberry juice with ice in cocktail shaker. Shake well, then strain into a chilled glass with ice and garnish with orange peel.

COSMOPOLITAN

Serves 1

Combine 1 shot of vodka, 1 shot of triple sec, 3 shots of cranberry juice and 1 tablespoon of lime juice with ice in a cocktail shaker. Shake and strain into a chilled cocktail glass.

GIN CUP

Recipe by Alex Thorp, Fifteen London

- 600ml gin
- ¼ cinnamon stick
- 8 x 2cm sliver ginger
- 4 pinches of camomile flowers (tea will do)
- 1 vanilla pod
- 12 fennel seeds
- 12 oregano leaves
- 8 juniper seeds
- 8 basil leaves
- 4 small sage leaves
- 12 rosemary leaves
- Zest of 2 lemons
- Zest of 1½ oranges
- 4 strips of grapefruit zest
- 8 tsp sugar
- 180ml of a sweet wine such as moscato or muscatel
- Mint and sliced seasonal fruit, such as lemons, limes, strawberries, apples, melons and cucumbers, and ice, to serve

1 In a clean, sterilised 1-litre jar, add all the ingredients except the sugar and sweet wine. Seal the jar and leave it at room temperature for 1–2 weeks, or until the flavour becomes pronounced. Strain the mixture through muslin.
2 Add the sweet wine and sugar, and stir to dissolve sugar. Transfer gin mixture to a clean bottle with a good seal. Store in the fridge (the wine will oxidise after about 2 weeks if left unsealed or out of the fridge).
3 To serve, mix 1 part infused gin to 3 parts lemonade, then add sliced fruit and ice cubes.

LONG ISLAND ICED TEA

Serves 1

Combine ½ shot of white tequila, ½ shot of white rum, ½ shot of vodka, ½ shot of gin and 2 tbsp of fresh lemon juice with ice in a cocktail shaker. Shake and strain into a chilled glass with ice and top up with Coke.

CUBA LIBRE

Serves 1

Pour 1 shot golden rum over ice in a highball glass. Squeeze in a wedge of lime and top up with Coke.

NEGRONI

CITRON PRESSE

NEGRONI
Serves 1

Combine 1 shot each of Campari, gin and sweet vermouth with ice in a cocktail shaker. Stir and strain into a chilled glass. Garnish with a twist of orange peel.

CITRON PRESSE

For a classic citron pressé, squeeze fresh lemons into glasses with sugar to taste and ice, and top up with water.

FIERY GINGER BEER
Serves 2

- 4 shots of chilli vodka (see page 156)
- Angostura bitters
- 500ml ginger beer
- Ice cubes

1 Mix the vodka, a few dashes of bitters and the ginger beer together in a jug. Fill two glasses halfway with ice then pour over the cocktail and serve.

GIN FIZZ
Serves 1

Rub cut lemon around rim of tumblers, then twist glass upside down in sugar. Add 2 generous shots of gin, juice of 2 lemons, 2 teaspoons of sugar and 1 egg white with ice in cocktail shaker and shake well. Pour into glasses, top up with soda and garnish with lemon slices.

BLOODY MARIA
Beware: this is strong!
Serves 2

- 4 shots tequila
- 300ml tomato juice
- Few dashes of Tabasco sauce, to taste
- Few dashes of worcestershire sauce, to taste
- Zest and juice of 2 limes
- 1–2 tbsp celery salt, to serve
- 1 fresh red chilli, 1 celery stalk and ice cubes, to serve

1 Pour the tequila, tomato juice, Tabasco and worcestershire sauce into a jug, then add the lime zest and juice. Give it a stir, have a taste and add adjust the flavours as you like. Chill it in the fridge.
2 Tip the celery salt onto a small plate, then halve and deseed your red chilli. Run one of the halves around the rims of your glasses, then dip them into the celery salt till coated. Add some ice to each glass, stir your Bloody Maria mix, divide it between glasses and garnish each with half a chilli and celery stalk.

PEACHY ICED TEA
Serves 4-6

- 2 Assam tea bags
- 3 tbsp sugar syrup
- 2 peaches, stoned and sliced

1 Place tea bags in a jug, and pour over 1 litre of boiling water. Leave to steep till desired strength. Remove tea bags, stir in sugar syrup, add peaches and chill till needed. Serve with lots of ice.

MANGO COOLER
Black salt is a pinkish Indian salt added to drinks for its cooling properties.
Recipe by Deep Mohan Singh Arneja
Serves 4

- 2 green mangoes, peeled, stoned and roughly chopped
- 90ml lime juice
- 3 tbsp caster sugar
- ½ tsp each black salt
- ½ tsp cumin powder
- Small bunch of mint, leaves picked
- 4 green cardamom pods, seeds only

1 Boil a pan of water. Add the mango and simmer for 20 minutes, until soft. Drain and cool. Put mango in a blender with 1 litre of water, a pinch of black pepper and all the other ingredients and blitz. Serve over ice with lime wedges.

FRAPPE

FRAPPE

Serves 1

- 1 heaped tsp Nescafé
- 1 heaped tsp sugar
- 1 glass iced water
- A dash of cold milk (optional)

1 Combine coffee, sugar and water with ice in a cocktail shaker. Shake well, then pour into a glass, adding milk if desired.

DIRTY MARTINI

Serves 1

Shake 2 shots of chilled gin or vodka, a dash of dry vermouth and ½ tbsp of brine from an olive or gherkin jar with ice in a cocktail shaker. Strain into a chilled cocktail glass and garnish with a green olive or gherkin, depending on which brine you used for your cocktail.

TEQUILA SUNRISE

Serves 1

Pour 1 shot of tequila and 3 shots of orange juice into a highball glass with ice. Stir, then add ½ shot of grenadine slowly and garnish with an orange slice.

PLANTERS PUNCH

Serves 1

Shake 1 shot each of dark and light rum, juice of 1 lime, ½ shot of triple sec, juice of ½ orange, a dash of grenadine, a dash of sugar syrup with ice in a cocktail shaker. Strain into a glass with ice. Top up with soda and garnish with orange slices.

SIDECAR

Serves 1

Rub cut lemon around the top of a glass then twist in saucer of sugar. Shake 1 shot each of brandy and triple sec and 2 tablespoons of lemon juice with ice in a cocktail shaker. Pour into a chilled tumbler and garnish with lemon peel.

PEAR CAIPIRINHA

Serves 2

- 2 shots cachaça (see note)
- Juice of 2 limes
- Small handful of mint leaves
- Handful of roughly crushed ice, plus extra to serve (optional)
- 200ml organic apple & pear cordial

1 Blitz the cachaça, lime juice, mint leaves and ice together. Transfer to glasses, top up with the cordial and serve straight or with crushed ice.
Note Cachaça is a clear Brazilian spirit made from sugarcane.

FLAVOURED SALT

FLAVOURED SALT

Keep this to hand to add serious oomph to meat, fish and stews.

Makes 250g

- 250g sea salt flakes
- 4 large dried chillies, stalks removed, or the zest from 2 large lemons

1 Add salt to a food processor or pestle and mortar. Add the chillies and blitz or bash until you've got a fairly fine flavoured salt. You can easily substitute herbs such as rosemary or thyme as flavouring for your salt.

SUGAR SYRUP

This is a good staple to have for use in desserts and drinks. Combine 200g sugar and 100ml cold water in a small saucepan over medium heat. Bring to boil and when the sugar has dissolved completely, remove from heat and allow to cool before transferring to a small bottle or jar. You can also make flavoured syrups by adding herbs and spices like mint, lemon verbena, cinnamon and cloves.

TARATOR

For a Lebanese-style snack, smear this garlicky dip on bread, add some grilled meat and a bit of salad or some mint.

Makes about 12 servings

- 6 garlic cloves, peeled
- 400g cold mashed potato
- 125ml vegetable oil

1 With a mortar and pestle, bash the garlic to a paste with a pinch of salt. Blend the garlic into the potato, then beat in as much oil as you need to make a slick purée. It should be firm, but just spreadable. Season to taste with salt.

SALSA PICANTE

Recipe from Jamie's Italian

- 6 yellow cherry tomatoes, quartered
- 6 red cherry tomatoes, quartered
- 6 baby plum tomatoes, quartered
- 6 plum tomatoes, deseeded and cut into strips
- 2 garlic cloves, finely chopped
- Large handful of basil leaves, sliced
- 80ml olive oil
- Juice of ½ lemon

1 Combine all ingredients, then season to taste with salt and black pepper. Serve with grilled meats and fish.

MINT SAUCE

Essential with roast lamb.

- 1 large bunch of mint, leaves picked
- 25g caster sugar
- 45ml white wine vinegar
- Extra-virgin olive oil

1 Add mint leaves to a liquidiser with 30ml boiling water, sugar, vinegar and a pinch of salt and pepper. Blitz to desired texture, season and drizzle with olive oil. This needs to be acidic enough to cut the richness of roast lamb, so add more vinegar as necessary.

BECHAMEL SAUCE

Makes about 1 litre

- 1 litre milk
- 2 bay leaves
- ½ tsp allspice berries
- 110g butter
- 120g plain flour
- 45g grated parmesan cheese
- ½ tsp grated nutmeg

1 Heat the milk, bay leaves and allspice in a saucepan to a simmer but don't let it boil. In another pan, melt the butter, then add the flour, stirring for about 5 minutes, until smooth. Slowly ladle the milk into the flour mixture (discarding bay and allspice), and whisk constantly until the sauce thickens. Remove the pan from the heat and, when slightly cooled, stir in the cheese and nutmeg.

SPICED PLUM CHUTNEY

PICKLED COURGETTES

SPICED PLUM CHUTNEY

Makes 500ml

- 1 tbsp vegetable oil
- 4 shallots, peeled and sliced
- 3 bay leaves
- 1 cinnamon stick
- 5 cloves
- ½ tsp ground allspice
- ½ tsp ground ginger
- 1kg mixed plums, stoned and chopped
- 400g brown sugar
- Zest and juice of 1 orange
- 300–400ml cider vinegar

1 Following the instructions in step one of the red-hot pickled chillies recipe, prepare a 500ml pickling jar.
2 Heat the vegetable oil in a saucepan that's big enough to hold all the ingredients. Add the shallots and cook gently over a low heat until softened and golden-brown. Add the bay leaves, cinnamon, cloves, allspince and ginger, fry for a minute, then stir in the plums. Add the sugar and orange zest. Pour the juice into a measuring jug and top up to the 450ml mark with cider vinegar. Add to the pan and bring to the boil, then simmer slowly until most of the water has evaporated and the chutney

is reduced and thick, stirring it every now and then as it cooks.
3 Spoon the chutney into a sterilised jar while everything's still nice and hot. Wipe the rim of the jar and seal it. Leave to cool and store in a cupboard for a few weeks before eating.

PICKLED COURGETTES

Makes 1.5kg

- 6 garlic cloves, sliced
- 250ml extra-virgin olive oil
- 250ml vegetable oil
- 1kg mixed yellow and green courgettes, washed
- 5–6 sprigs of mint
- 1 red chilli, chopped

Pickling liquid

- 1 litre cider vinegar or white wine vinegar
- 1 tbsp salt

1 Place the pickling liquid ingredients in a big pan along with 1 litre of water and bring to the boil. Put the garlic in a clean mixing bowl and pour the oils on top. Slice courgettes into quarters or halves lengthways, depending on their size, and then across into thick slices. Put the courgettes, mint and chilli in the boiling liquid and simmer for about 3 minutes.

2 Lift the courgettes, mint and chillies out with a slotted spoon, gently shaking to get rid of any excess liquid. Transfer to the garlic oil, season with salt and pepper, and quickly spoon the oil and courgettes into sterilised jars before they lose too much heat. Wipe the rims of the jars so there's no oil on them, then seal the tops, turn the jars upside down and leave to cool. Turn right-way up when the jars are cold, and store in the cupboard for a couple of weeks before eating.

TOMATO SAUCE

Add other ingredients such as fresh herbs or seafood to this basic recipe. Otherwise, use it as a base for pizzas, as a pasta sauce or simply drizzle it over grilled or baked fish and chicken.

Makes about 500ml

- 5 tbsp olive oil
- 1 garlic clove, peeled and finely diced
- 1 tsp dried oregano
- 1kg plum tomatoes, peeled, deseeded and finely chopped

1 Heat the olive oil in a frying pan over a medium heat. Add the garlic and oregano and sauté for 5 minutes or until softened. Add the tomatoes and season to taste with salt and pepper. Simmer for 40 minutes, stirring occasionally.

SOUTH INDIAN PUMPKIN PICKLE

TUNA BUTTER

SOUTH INDIAN PUMPKIN PICKLE

Makes 1 litre

- 30ml vegetable oil
- 1 tsp each mustard and fenugreek seeds
- 2 medium red onions, finely sliced
- 3 garlic cloves, grated
- 2.5cm-piece of fresh ginger, grated
- 1 tbsp each ground coriander, ground cumin and turmeric
- 400g tin of chopped tomatoes
- Grated zest and juice of 6 limes
- 350–450ml cider vinegar
- 2 green chillies, halved and deseeded
- 500g deseeded pumpkin
- 1½ tsp salt
- 250g brown sugar

1 Heat the oil in a saucepan that's big enough to hold all ingredients. When smoking, add mustard and fenugreek seeds – they should start to pop. Stir in the onion, garlic and ginger, turn the heat down and cook slowly, stirring, till the mixture is dark brown and fragrant. Add the spices, stir-fry for a minute or so, then add the tomatoes. Bring to a boil and simmer gently for a few minutes. 2 Add the lime zest. Pour the lime juice into a measuring jug and top up to 500ml with vinegar. Pour into the pan,

add chillies and pumpkin, and bring back to the boil. When pumpkin is just cooked, lift it out with a spoon into a clean mixing bowl and set aside. Add salt and sugar to the pan, and cook till the liquid is reduced and thick. Fold the pumpkin back in, making sure it's hot before turning the heat off. Spoon into sterilised jars while everything's still hot. Seal the jars and leave to cool. It will be ready to eat in a few weeks' time.

RAITA

Combine ½ grated large cucumber, 250g plain Greek-style yoghurt, 1 teaspoon of extra-virgin olive oil and a pinch of ground cumin. Season to taste, then serve with curries.

SHORTCRUST PASTRY

A basic recipe for all types of pies.

- 250g plain flour
- 125g cold butter, diced
- 1 egg
- 3–5 tbsp cold water

1 Put the flour, butter and a pinch of salt into a food processor and blend till the mixture resembles breadcrumbs. With the machine still running, add in

the egg. Slowly add enough water to make a soft dough. Form the dough into a disk, wrap in clingfilm and refrigerate for at least 30 minutes before using according to the recipe instructions.

MANGO JAM

This condiment for ham also can be made with papayas.

- 3 ripe mangoes, seed removed, flesh cut into 2cm cubes
- 225g brown sugar
- 1 cinnamon stick

1 Place all ingredients in a saucepan with 250ml of water and cook over a medium heat for 25–30 minutes, or until the sugar has dissolved and the sauce begins to thicken. Allow to cool. Place in a jar and store in the refrigerator for up to a week.

TUNA BUTTER

Delicious on toast.

- 2 tins good quality tuna in olive oil, drained
- 210g butter
- 2 anchovy fillets, chopped
- 1 tbsp capers, drained

1 Blend ingredients in a food processor till smooth. Serve with Italian flatbread.

RASPBERRY JAM

RASPBERRY JAM

This makes quite a runny jam.

Makes 1.2kg

- 1kg raspberries
- 800g golden caster sugar
- ½ lemon, juiced
- 1 vanilla pod, split opened (optional)

1 Put the raspberries in a large pan along with the lemon juice and simmer very gently for about 5 minutes, stirring. When the juice begins to flow from the fruit, bring to the boil, add the vanilla pod and boil gently for 5 minutes. Warm the sugar in a heatproof bowl in a low oven and add to the fruit stirring until it dissolve. Bring it back to the boil for 2 minutes. Take off the heat and spoon off any scum. Remove the vanilla pod. Leave to stand for 15 minutes, transfer to a sterilised jar and refrigerate.

COFFEE CARAMEL

This is lovely served with baked cheesecake or over vanilla ice cream.

- 80g dark brown sugar
- 1 shot strong espresso
- 70g unsalted butter
- 65ml double cream

1 Stir ingredients in a pan over a low heat till sugar dissolves. Boil for 3–4 minutes. Cool slightly and stir before serving.

CAESAR SALAD DRESSING

Recipe from Jamie's Italian

Whisk 100ml whole-egg mayonnaise, 1 tablespoon of crème fraîche, 1 finely chopped garlic clove, 2 finely chopped anchovy fillets with juice of ½ lemon and season to taste.

TOMATO CHUTNEY

Makes about 700g

- Olive oil
- 2 red onions, finely chopped
- 3 garlic cloves, finely sliced
- Thumb-sized piece of ginger, peeled and finely chopped
- 1 tbsp black mustard seeds
- 4 cardamom pods, crushed
- 6 cloves
- 1 cinnamon stick
- 1kg ripe cherry tomatoes, halved
- 300g light brown sugar
- 400ml red wine vinegar
- 2 red chillies, sliced

1 In a saucepan, heat a little olive oil and sweat the onion, garlic and ginger for about 10 minutes, until soft. Add the spices and toast for a few minutes, until the mustard seeds start to pop. Add the tomatoes, sugar, vinegar and chillies, and bring to a simmer. Let it tick away for an hour or so till it's jammy. Transfer to sterilised jars, place in the fridge, and keep for up to 2 months.

CHIMICHURRI SAUCE

of lemon juice and taste it again. Keep adding little drizzles of oil and lemon until you get the taste and consistency you're after. Transfer to a sterilised jar, then refrigerate until needed.

SCOTCH BONNET SAUCE

This chilli sauce is insanely potent, so use with care. It will keep in the fridge for up to three months.
Makes 190g

- 15 scotch bonnet chillies
- 2 red wine vinegar
- 2 tbsp olive oil

1 Wearing rubber gloves, deseed and chop chillies and transfer to a blender. Add 2 tbsp sea salt and blitz to a fine pulp. Add vinegar and oil, blitz again, then transfer to a sterilised jar and refrigerate.

MEAT RAGU

Makes about 1.2 litres

- 4 tbsp olive oil
- 2 medium-sized onions, diced
- 2 garlic cloves, finely chopped
- 2 celery stalks, diced
- 3 tbsp finely chopped parsley
- 1 tsp dried oregano
- 1 sprig of fresh thyme
- 1kg lean minced beef
- 125ml red wine
- 1 x 400g can chopped tomatoes
- 1 tbsp tomato purée
- 1 tsp cinnamon
- 1 bay leaf

1 Heat 3 tablespoons of olive oil in a saucepan over a medium heat, and sauté the onions, garlic, celery, parsley, oregano and thyme for 5 minutes, till softened. Transfer to a bowl.
2 Add the remaining olive oil to the saucepan and sauté the beef, stirring constantly, for 10 minutes, until it's browned. Add the wine, tomatoes, tomato purée, cinnamon and bay leaf. Season to taste with sea salt and black pepper and sauté for another 5 minutes. Return the onion, garlic and celery mixture to the saucepan and stir well to combine. Simmer the sauce for 45-60 minutes, until it thickens.

CHIMICHURRI SAUCE

Makes about 250ml

- 120ml olive oil
- 60ml red wine vinegar
- 1 onion, finely chopped
- 2 tomatoes, peeled, deseeded and chopped
- 3 garlic cloves, finely chopped
- 1 small handful of chopped parsley
- 1 tsp each of dried oregano, chilli powder, paprika and ground cumin
- 1 bay leaf, finely chopped

1 Whisk the olive oil with the vinegar. Stir in the other ingredients and season with salt and pepper. Mix well, then let it marinate for 2 hours before serving with steaks or grilled fish. This will keep in the fridge for up to 5 days.

PESTO

Makes 170g

- ¼ garlic clove, chopped
- 3 large handfuls of basil leaves
- 1 handful of pine nuts, lightly toasted
- 1 good handful of grated parmesan
- Extra-virgin olive oil
- Juice of 1-2 lemons

1 Place the garlic in a pestle and mortar or a food processor. Pound or pulse the garlic with the basil, then, when minced, add the pine nuts and pound or pulse again. When blitzed but still with a good rustic consistency, transfer to a mixing bowl. Stir in half the parmesan, then add a little olive oil, just enough to get the right consistency - semi-wet but still firm. Taste, season with sea salt and black pepper and the rest of the cheese. Add some more oil and a little squeeze

PICKLED CHILLIES

HOLLANDAISE SAUCE

PICKLED CHILLIES

Makes an 800ml jar

- 400ml white vinegar, plus extra
- 1 tsp peppercorns
- 1 tsp fennel seeds
- 1½ tbsp salt
- 1½ tbsp golden caster sugar
- About 200g assorted chillies
- 2-3 bay leaves

1 Place the vinegar in a saucepan. Add 400ml water and then another good splash of vinegar. Add the peppercorns and fennel seeds and place on the heat. Add the salt and golden caster sugar. Allow to simmer for about 5 minutes.
2 Wearing gloves if you're dealing with particularly hot varieties, slice the chillies in half lengthways and remove the seeds. Be careful none of them ping up towards your eyes! Push the chillies in your sterilised jar, one by one, until they are well packed. Push the bay between the chillies and make sure it all looks nice through the glass.
3 Pour the pickling liquid into the jar of chillies. It's important to fill the jar pretty close to the top because, as the air bubbles rise to the top, the level of the liquid will fall and you want the chillies to be submerged. Seal the jar while everything's still hot. Leave to cool down, and then open and enjoy after a couple of weeks

HOLLANDAISE SAUCE

- 150g unsalted butter
- 2 large eggs yolks
- 1 dessertspoon white wine vinegar
- Lemon wedges, for squeezing

1 Get a saucepan and a heatproof mixing bowl that will sit stably over the pan. Half-fill the pan with water and bring to a simmer. Turn down the heat as low as it can go but still have the water simmering.
2 Meanwhile, place the butter in a medium-sized pan over a low heat, so it starts to melt but doesn't burn. When butter has melted, take it off the heat.
3 Place the egg yolks in your heatproof mixing bowl, which you should then place over the pan of just-simmering water. It's important that the pan is on a low heat, or the eggs will scramble.
4 Using a balloon whisk, start to beat your eggs, then whisk in your white wine vinegar. Keep whisking, and then start adding the melted butter by slowly drizzling it in, whisking all the time, till all the butter has been incorporated. The result should be a smooth, thick sauce. Season carefully with salt and black pepper, and loosen if necessary with little squeezes of lemon juice. Keep tasting the sauce until the flavour is to your liking.

HERBY MAYONNAISE

- Bunch of chives
- Bunch of tarragon, leaves picked
- Bunch of mint, leaves picked
- 500ml olive oil
- 1 tsp dijon mustard
- 1 egg yolk
- 3 tbsp good-quality wine vinegar

1 Blitz herbs and 100ml olive oil in a food processor until smooth. Put mustard and egg yolk into a bowl on a damp tea towel to stop it slipping and whisk while drizzling in remaining oil. Whisk in vinegar, season to taste, then whisk in herby oil bit by bit. Taste and adjust seasoning or vinegar as necessary. Refrigerate for up to 3 days.
Note If you've split it, don't worry. Try adding a few tablespoons of boiling water as you whisk. If it doesn't come back, whisk an egg yolk and some mustard in another bowl, then whisk in your split mayo bit by bit.

 # yearbook index

Editor
Andy Harris

Managing editor
Paul Dring

Art director
Adrienne Pitts

Deputy editor
Holly O'Neill

Editor at large
Jamie Oliver

Recipes
Pete Begg, April Bloomfield, Antonio Carluccio, Gennaro Contaldo, Rodney Dunn, Abigail Fawcett, Laura Fyfe, Andy Harris, Mark Hix, Jules Hunt, Anna Jones, Adam Perry Lang, Paul Levy, Greg Malouf, Kate McCullough, Deep Mohan Singh Arneja, Jamie Oliver, Andrew Parkinson, Bernard Perrier, Nicolo Ravida, Stéphane Réynaud, Ginny Rolfe, Georgie Socratous, Hui Nei Yang

Photography
David Loftus, Tara Fisher, Dan Jones, Lisa Linder, William Meppem, Myles New, Con Poulos, Sam Stowell, Karen Thomas, Simon Wheeler

Recipe testing
Siobhan Boyle, Abigail Fawcett, Laura Fyfe, Anna Jones, Kate McCullough, Rebecca Rauter, Ginny Rolfe, Georgie Socratous, Phillippa Spence

Advertising
Mark Rice & Ruth White
+20 7395 6000

Jamie Oliver Ltd
CEO John Jackson
Managing director Tara Donovan
Finance manager John Dewar
Accounts manager Campbell Gower
Legal & business affairs Melissa Royde

Subscriptions Jamie Magazine, 800 Guillat Avenue, Kent Science Park, Sittingbourne, Kent ME9 8GU
01795 414951, jamiemagazine@servicehelpline.co.uk

Australia, New Zealand, Canada and South Africa distribution: IPG, PO Box 393, Belmont, WA, Australia 6984; +61 8 9362 4134, wa@ipgonline.cc
Newstrade distributor: NDD Pty Ltd, Building 5, 190-196 Bourke Rd, Alexandria, NSW, Australia 2015; +61 2 9381 3100

International distribution (excluding Australia, New Zealand, Canada and South Africa) by Seymour International Ltd, 2 East Poultry Avenue, London EC1A 9PT, +44 20 7429 1000

PEFC
PEFC/16-33-275
This magazine is printed on paper produced from sustainable managed forests accredited by the PEFC (Programme for the Endorsement of Forest Certification schemes; pefc.org)

Editor's choice

Here's a chance to buy a 12-bottle case of the wines we've recommended at the beginning of the chapters in this book. We love them with our recipes, and hope you do too

JAMIE MAGAZINE WINE CLUB

HALF PRICE!
WAS £121.88
NOW
£60.94

PREFER 6 BOTTLES?
Snap up a 6-bottle case for
£39.99
(worth £74.94)

naked wines

We've chosen fantastic wines to go with recipes across each chapter of our yearbook. There's a crisp albariño for an apéritif, spicy Rhône red to sip with soups, an Italian red for pasta, a fish-friendly classic chardonnay, grenache that's great with meat, an award-winning dessert wine, and even a champagne for celebrations. We think they make the perfect case for any feast!

- Exclusive to readers of the Jamie Magazine Recipe Yearbook 2009/10
- Worth £121.88, but you can buy 12-bottle case today for just £60.94. That's half-price!
- Wines are covered by a 100% money back guarantee
- NEXT DAY delivery is standard for only £4.99

Wine in this case

1 x 2008 Mar de Viñas Albariño
2 x 2007 La Croix du Chêne
2 x 2009 Arabella Chenin Blanc
2 x 2008 Milani Montepulciano d'Abruzzo
2 x 2008 Canepa Classico Chardonnay
1 x 2008 Domaine Cristia Vin de Pays Grenache
1 x 2006 Domaine Cristia Muscat de Beaumes de Venise
1 x NV Champagne Moutard

HOW TO ORDER

Visit nakedwines.com/jamieyearbook
or call 01603 281 800

This offer is exclusive to readers of the Jamie Magazine Recipe Yearbook 2009/10 aged 18 and over. Case offer and wines subject to availability and delivery to UK residents only. One case per person and per houshold. For full terms and conditions, please visit nakedwines.com